Transnational Crime

Transnational Crime

Edited by

Jay Albanese

de Sitter Publications

INTERNATIONAL STUDIES IN SOCIAL SCIENCE

Series Editor
S. Ishwaran

VOLUME 10

Transnational Crime

Edited by

Jay Albanese

CANADIAN CATALOGUING IN PUBLICATION DATA

Transnational Crime
Edited by Jay Albanese
ISBN 1-897160-05-4
International Studies in Social Science
ISSN 1497-9616

Cover design: de Sitter Publications

de Sitter Publications
104 Consumers Dr., Whitby, ON,
L1N 1C4, Canada

http://www.desitterpublications.com
sales@desitterpublications.com

Contents

Introduction

TRANSNATIONAL CRIME

*Jay Albanese**

Transnational crime will characterize the twenty-first century much in the same way that earlier technological developments changed the face of crime in the twentieth century. Consider the impact of the invention of the automobile, telephone, and computer on social life and crime during the 1900s. Compare that to what we have already seen in the early years of the twenty-first century with the rise of global Internet access, the collapse of political barriers to international travel, and the general expansion of communication to a truly global scale. These changes in society and technology are already having dramatic impacts on crime.

This volume assembles seven contributions on important dimensions of transnational crime from authors in three different countries. Many of these issues were incomprehensible in the recent past. The topics include trafficking in human beings, intellectual property theft, commercial sexual exploitation of children, how we organize the law enforcement response to transnational crime and terrorism, and how we teach and understand the methodology of different cultures and account for divergent perspectives on social problems.

Trafficking in human beings, the subject of three studies in this volume, has been poorly understood thus far due to a lack of primary source information. This volume fills this void with a study by **Dina Siegel** dealing with human trafficking, coercion, voluntariness, and the legal and illegal sex trade in the Netherlands. Professor Siegel's interviews with the

* Virginia Commonwealth University and National Institute of Justice, 810 Seventh St., NW, Washington, DC 20531, USA, (justiceworks@yahoo.com).

women caught in these competing commercial, political, and social forces offer unique insight into the dynamics behind prostitution there.

The commercial sexual exploitation of children has gained attention in recent years and the study that I describe in this volume organizes both the existing data and experience. It demonstrates how the cycle of child sexual exploitation operates and what interventions are needed to have a meaningful impact on this conduct, as its crosses the boundaries of human trafficking, pornography, child abuse, prostitution, and sex tourism.

Hedieh Nasheri's contribution on intellectual property theft documents the unique nature of intellectual property theft as both an end in itself and as a support mechanism for both organized crime and terrorist groups. She finds evidence of networking among criminal groups across borders, a process facilitated by transnational technological and financial exchanges. She provides a systematic overview of the strengths and weaknesses of current efforts to curtail this form of transnational crime.

Heather Clawson, Kevonne Small, Ellen Go, and Bradley Myles conducted a fascinating study to determine what social/psychological/legal services exist for victim of human trafficking, and what services do these victims really need? They carried out a national telephone survey in the United States, and held focus groups with service providers and trafficking victims. The gaps and barriers to effective services for trafficking victims are well documented.

The true extent of human trafficking is unknown. **Jay Albanese, Jennifer Schrock Donnelly, and Talene Kelegian** make an effort to develop hard data through an analysis of news reports of police actions related to trafficking in 18 large border cities in the United States. Their study finds remarkably few cases, but the authors address this issue and also describe what can be concluded about the circumstances of trafficking based on the cases they found.

Research methodology is a fundamental skill because it provides the background needed to obtain valid and reliable knowledge. **Rosemary Barberet** documents that comparative methodology is rarely taught in criminology and it is rarely addressed in textbooks. She makes the case that the relatively low volume and poor quality of some comparative research in criminology and criminal justice may be due to the failure to prepare students to conduct research in international settings.

The law enforcement response to transnational crime and terrorism is crucial to provide meaning to national and international laws and conventions directed toward these crimes. **William McDonald** documents how failures of cooperation with the U.S. law enforcement and intelligence community may be a larger problem than cooperation in the international law enforcement community—comparing the American and European approaches to transnational law enforcement cooperation.

The research reported in this volume adds both new data and insightful analysis to the growing literature on emerging forms of transnational crime and research. You are invited to correspond with the authors of this work so that research efforts in this area will continue to move forward.

Chapter 1

RECENT TRENDS IN WOMEN TRAFFICKING AND VOLUNTARY PROSTITUTION: RUSSIAN-SPEAKING SEX-WORKERS IN THE NETHERLANDS

*Dina Siegel**

Cultural and economic globalization has promoted the spread of old and the emergence of new forms of organized crime activities, women trafficking being one of them. A number of organizations have reported on the involvement of organized crime groups in the smuggling and trafficking of women around the world.[1] The phenomenon is usually presented by the media in stories of misery and shattered illusions: innocent girls, cheated by criminals and put to work as prostitutes, are forced to live without documents or rights in foreign countries where they have no one to turn to. Organized crime is usually mentioned in these stories: they are not only about violent and sophisticated traffickers who kidnap, sell and force young women to travel abroad, but also about complex criminal organizations involved in the exploitation and mistreatment of young women in the receiving countries. The victims themselves are usually described as passive and naïve girls, whose only wish is to escape from the tentacles of these criminal organizations and go home.

In recent years, information about the dangers and risks to women who get trapped in the networks of criminals has been widely distributed by numerous NGO's and other interest groups, and this information has reached the most remote towns and villages around the world. Different public and semi-governmental groups have warned women about the

---

* Vrije Universiteit, Amsterdam, De Boelelaan 1105, 1081 HV Amsterdam, The Netherlands (d.siegel@rechten.vu.nl).

horrors facing them when they are sold as slaves abroad. There are now many Internet sites, information flyers, reports in the media and in films on the possible dangers of working abroad.[2] Representatives of the Ministry of Internal Affairs of the Russian Federation confirmed that the majority of Russian-speaking sex-workers in foreign countries were aware of the fact that they would be involved in prostitution before they left Russia.[3] The argument that most of the women in the former Soviet Union are naïve and ignorant of what to expect, is no longer convincing.

According to a number of reports and articles, the traditional approach used by traffickers to recruit women for the sex industry rested on simple deception: the likely candidates were promised jobs as translators, dancers, waitresses or nannies.[4] In the last years, according to some sources, the traffickers have perfected their lies. When they offer jobs abroad, they are now able to show fake contracts or other documents to convince the women of the sincerity of their proposals (Hughes and Denisova 2001; Hughes 2002). According to the American NGO MiraMed, criminals in Russia have gone so far as to set up "career days" in institutes and universities, with promises of profitable work abroad. In some of our cases on trafficking in Turkey we found that "dancing schools" or "oriental dance courses" were advertised, which attracted especially young girls (Siegel and Yesilgoz 2003). According to these sources, criminal organizations are creative in finding new tricks to get a hold of young women. Anti-trafficking organizations have warned Russian women against this kind of manipulation and the latest criminal methods (Hughes and Denisova 2001).

On the other hand, the economic interests of women who can hardly make ends meet in their own countries and are attracted by opportunities to make quick money in the West in order to support their families and save for a better future, are rarely mentioned. But it is precisely this economic choice that appears to be crucial in their decision to become sex-workers abroad. They have discovered that they can earn their monthly salary in just one day of work as a prostitute; they have been told by friends who already live in the West about the possibilities and risks; they make their own calculations and finally decide to travel abroad to become a sex-worker. Their decision can be explained as the result of economic instability and a high level of unemployment in their home countries, but it is still their own choice to improve their financial situation. Nobody, certainly no criminal organization, forced them to make this decision.

There are ongoing debates on the differences between trafficking and prostitution and on the differences between forced and voluntary prostitution. The role of organized crime depends on these differences. When they describe the position of women who were kidnapped, raped and forced into prostitution, criminologists usually look for an explanation in the context of organized crime. However, when independent and self-supporting women choose the oldest profession in the world as their business, organized crime plays a marginal role at best. But the idea of prostitution as business and voluntary prostitution as a new, post-reform trend is prevalent among many women from the former Soviet Union who came to Western Europe—and to the Netherlands in particular—to fulfil their economic hopes and dreams.

For more than seventy years, Russian-speaking women were part of a culture where sex was taboo. The reforms and especially the opening of the borders completely changed their attitudes towards sex, men, and themselves.[5] They view the Netherlands as a place of "luxury," an idea based on old, pre-reform perceptions of the West, and in this country they expect to not only earn more money, but also enjoy the European lifestyle that was so highly appreciated in the former Soviet Union.[6] The Netherlands has always had the reputation of a tolerant and liberal country, a place of "live and let live," where there are many opportunities to engage in any kind of business, including the sex-business.

In 2000, however, Dutch legislation on prostitution went through some major changes, which emphasized the legal and voluntary character of the profession. Prostitution was almost always tolerated by the Dutch authorities, but never before did it reach the status of an ordinary profession like any other, with all the rights and benefits involved. Together with new developments concerning prostitution as a "normal" profession, other more negative effects became clear: non-European women were banned from working in legal brothels and, as a consequence, they disappeared into the illegal circuit where, allegedly, they became easy victims of criminal organizations and new forms of women trafficking. Russian-speaking women are now forced to work outside the legal framework if they want to stay in the country. This makes them vulnerable to illegal entrepreneurs and various forms of criminal activities. At least, that is the hypothesis, but is that really what is happening? Is it possible that, on the contrary, the adverse circumstances of being unable to work in a regular legal context pushed young, ambitious Russian-speaking women to look for alternatives and to develop an illegal but very successful independent trade in the Dutch sex-trade industry?

In this chapter I hope to answer the following questions:

- Are prostitution and women trafficking really connected to organized crime as it is usually presented in the media?
- Did the new law in the Netherlands change the character of voluntary prostitution?
- What are the consequences of these changes for non-European, in this case Russian-speaking, sex-workers in the illegal market?

The purpose of this chapter is to analyse the recent developments in women trafficking and prostitution, particularly in a Dutch-Russian context, and to present the data derived from my fieldwork in 2001-2002 among Russian-speaking sex-workers in the Netherlands. I will focus on the conditions, motives, organization and consequences of women trafficking and voluntary prostitution, with particular attention to the role of organized crime.

Background and Research Methods

Several attempts were recently made to gain insight into the developments in the world of illegal prostitution and its links to organized crime.[7] The main problem of qualitative research is that it is difficult, if not impossible, to get in touch with illegal prostitutes. First, it is unknown where they live and work; and secondly, they are now less open to talk about their situation than when they worked under the protection of legal brothel-owners. A few studies, however, achieved some success. One of them, conducted by the Verwey-Jonker Institute, on illegal and forced prostitution was published in 2002 (Goderie et al. 2002). From this report it appears that, one year after the introduction of the law, prostitutes without a legal status in the Netherlands were not only active in sectors that are difficult to control, such as street prostitution and the escort business, but also in window prostitution and in sex clubs, much like the situation before 2000. We are, however, still left with the question of what happens to those women who did leave the legal sex clubs. Did they end up in the hands of criminals? Studies on the "hidden" forms of prostitution mention criminal activities connected to prostitution, such as threats, blackmail, the weapons-trade, the drugs-trade, document forgery, and financial crimes (Daalder 2002:43). Supposedly there is a link between prostitution and organized crime in the form of women trafficking.

In 1999 and 2000 empirical research among Russian-speaking women and Turkish men was conducted with a purpose to gain insight into the motives, background, and new trends in women trafficking on the one hand, and various forms of voluntary prostitution on the other hand (Siegel and Yesilgoz 2003).[8] This was the first phase of a study on Russian-speaking prostitutes in the Netherlands within their own group. After the introduction of the Brothel Law in 2000, I continued my research on Russian-speaking sex workers, in an attempt to monitor the consequences of this law for Russian women. Focusing on the situation in the Netherlands, I analysed new studies and media reports in Russia and the Netherlands; I conducted interviews with different organizations, such as De Rode Draad[9] and the Dutch police; and gathered statistical information on human trafficking in general, and women trafficking in the Netherlands in particular. Conducting open interviews with prostitutes from the former Soviet Union, I used a "quasi-snowball" research method, in which the informants were not only asked about their own experiences, but also about the experiences of others. The most important results of the research were achieved by the method of participant observation. I visited several informants at their illegal "secret" places, where they received their clients, mainly in rented apartments, which they shared with other women. Two girls were running an "alternative medical clinic," in which they received clients for erotic massages and "other treatment," but most of the women were employed during the day as nannies, housekeepers, or at flower factories, while in the evening they worked in illegal brothels or as independent call-girls.

My findings are based on intensive contacts with ten informants: young Russian, Ukrainian, Armenian, Georgian, and Byelorussian women between 16 to 31 years old. Six of them had finished secondary and professional education and four were university graduates. Back in Russia, they were employed as a teacher, a translator, a doctor, an economist, a bank clerk, a model, etc. Most of them were unmarried, one was divorced and two were married to Russian men living in Russia with their children and parents. All of them came to work as prostitutes in the Netherlands voluntarily. In addition, I talked to fifteen other women. These conversations varied from several hours with the same informant on different occasions to short conversations at birthday parties or during mutual activities such as the celebration of the Russian New Year. All conversations were conducted in Russian, my own, native language. The information I gathered was extremely useful: the women told me their life-stories, with an emphasis on their problems in the former Soviet Union and in the Netherlands. They talked about their past, their families, their plans for the future and, of course, about their life and work in the Netherlands. They shared with me their ideas on Dutch prostitution policies and Dutch culture in general, on their clients and contacts with other Russian-speaking sex-workers and other people connected to their trade. They saw me as a compatriot who was far more familiar with the Netherlands than they were, and they often asked me for advice or information on Dutch habits and culture. Sometimes they asked me to translate letters or make telephone calls in Dutch for them, which I usually did.

Empirical research has its drawbacks: (a) the population is limited (problems of external validity); (b) press reports on women trafficking should be taken into the analysis (selectivity); (c) informants often provide unreliable information: they may lie, gossip, invent stories, change facts, and manipulate their identity. This problem is well-known in empirical research on deviant behaviour, and it takes time, patience, trust, and an involvement in the population under study. The strong points of this kind of research include direct observation and close contacts with informants and the possibility to demonstrate the discrepancy between the data provided by the informants and what is reported in the media; in other words, to redefine a phenomenon with the assistance of those actually involved, can help to debunk myths and stereotypes and thus bring us closer to reality.

"Russian" Prostitutes—Image and Reality

I divided the women with whom I had contacts during my research and/or whom I was told about by my informants into four categories:

1. call girls and escort services,
2. "Russian wives,"
3. street prostitutes, and
4. private illegal services.

The first group included Russian-speaking immigrant women who legally worked in sex clubs or as call girls. Most of them either had a residence permit or Dutch citizenship. The Russian-speaking women in the second group were married to or were living with Dutch men and occasionally worked as call girls or escort girls to earn their own money and gain some financial independence from their Dutch husbands. This group of "Russian wives" found it difficult to live with Dutch men, mainly because of cultural misunderstandings[10] (Siegel 2002:89-90). The third group included legal and illegal migrant prostitutes who worked the streets, most of them were addicted to drugs (mainly heroin). I found the fourth group the most interesting: these were women who were looking for alternative illegal ways to work as prostitutes in the Netherlands, in order to deal with the changes in the Dutch prostitution laws. I will focus specifically on this group: Russian-speaking women engaged in the illegal sex-business.

Early on during my fieldwork, I realized that the image of trafficked women who are forced to work as prostitutes under the threat of violence, did not fit the women I dealt with. Similar to my previous research on Russian-speaking women and Turkish men, I found that all my informants presented themselves as businesswomen, namely independent sex-workers. In the group of illegal sex-workers I distinguish two sub-groups: (1) women who had lived in the Netherlands for more than 5 years, were previously employed in brothels, but had to seek employment elsewhere as a result of the new regulations; and (2) newcomers who arrived after October 2000 to work as prostitutes.

Motives

The motives to become a prostitute in the Netherlands vary from the purely economic to a combination of economic and cultural reasons. This is typical of both categories, those who arrived before and after the introduction of the Brothel Law of 2000.

One of my informants, Svetlana (age 27), arrived in 1998:

> *I am an economist by profession, and I had a relatively good job in Minsk, but my salary was approximately 60 dollars per month. Working in a sex-club in Amsterdam I earned enough to help my parents and to save for the future. I could also afford all kinds of luxuries I never dreamt about before.*

Another motive most of my informants who came after 2000 emphasized during my fieldwork were the positive reports from Russian-speaking women in the Netherlands, who encouraged their friends to come and work there illegally.

Galina (age 22) completed her professional financial education, worked in a bank in Kiev and arrived in the Netherlands in June 2002:

> *My friend told me that in Holland I could earn a monthly salary in one day if I joined her and this was enough for me to make my decision. With two other girls we now rent a 7-room villa in a suburb of Amsterdam and each of us has her own clients.*

Ways of Travelling and the Role of Travel Agencies

The most popular way for women to travel from Russia is through travel agencies—often legitimate—and with the use of (usually) authentic documents. The women travel as tourists, but do not return from Europe.[11] My informants usually travelled alone, or in small groups of three women at most, but never as part of organized tourist trips, in order to "move freely and not be controlled by others." They carried the address of a contact person in the Netherlands (usually Russian or Dutch), provided by the travel agency where they booked their tickets. Later, upon their arrival in the Netherlands, the contact persons turned out to be brothel owners or private persons who either operated an illegal brothel, or mediated between different sex clubs. This was, however, no surprise to them and they hoped to find work in an expensive sex club, where they could earn more money. In some cases they realized that these contacts were unlike regular employers and that their demands were higher and the economic commitments much harder to fulfil than they had expected. Women who travelled privately, without the assistance of travel agencies, described the same pattern. They were given addresses of contacts in the Netherlands (often brothel owners) by friends who already worked there.

All my informants travelled by plane. All of them booked their tickets in one or another travel agency. The role of these agencies goes far beyond selling tickets. Traditionally, Russian criminals operate behind the facade of an employment agency, a travel agency, or modelling or matchmaking agencies. The last two, for example, are used to identify women looking for an opportunity to go abroad. Information is sometimes exchanged with criminal organisations (Highes and Denisova 2001). My informants, however, did not consider the people in the travel agencies to be “traffickers,” but rather “agents” or *organizatori* (“organizers” or “managers”). According to my informants *organizatori* are “businesspeople,” who do not necessarily belong to criminal organisations, but it is true that they rely on *krysha*, protection, which allows them to run their business. Without *krysha* no business can survive, according to the women, and they consider this phenomenon an inevitability in the unstable post-reform socioeconomic situation in the former Soviet Union.

Most of the women that I met paid for their own airline ticket and arranged their own visa and hotel reservation or private place to stay. Many were assisted by friends or acquaintances in the destination country beforehand. In a few cases they gave gifts to the organizers in the travel agency (gold chains, French perfume, and/or money) on top of the regular costs of their ticket and visa. One gave a bribe to a travel agent for “arranging” a place on an airplane, when no places were available for that particular flight. According to some informants, the organizers were people you could trust, at least as far as logistic support. They had more problems with the people who met them in the Netherlands.

On arrival in the Netherlands

As soon as the women arrived, they found themselves connected to a whole network of pimps, brothel owners and even their old friends, who now wanted payment for their assistance and contacts. In addition, they were sometimes asked to do things they were not ready for, such as group sex, extra long hours, etc.

> Irina (age 21), who arrived in 2001:
>
> *I don’t mind working extra hours, but I don’t want to give my money to these parasites around me. One can earn a lot of money in three illegal sectors: weapon, drugs and women. In all three you earn almost the same, but the first two are full of risks. Let these ‘tough guys’ deal with the risky things, and leave me alone.*

The first few months Irina worked for a brothel owner who "in spite of the new law and controls" was willing to employ her, but then she left the brothel and started work as a call girl, mostly "with the same regular clients," as she put it.

There are a few common features to all my informants: all women were aware of what their future job in the Netherlands entailed (or at least guessed what kind of work they were going to do). Secondly, when they were still in the former Soviet Union, they realized that they had the choice either to travel or not; in the Netherlands they found themselves tied to various dubious figures and under financial obligations. Thirdly, although they were willing to work as prostitutes, there were not always ready for the working conditions and the financial demands made on them.

It is usually assumed that exploitation of and violence against "trafficked women" is a result of their dependence on criminals who organize their trip, sometimes travel with them and eventually employ them in the sex industry. It appears from my fieldwork that these assumptions are far from accurate.

Natasha (29), arrived in 2001:

I came from Ukraine to the Netherlands to earn money. I travelled with another girl, who had a contact in Amsterdam: a Russian woman, called Ekaterina, married to a Dutchman. She got this contact from the travel agency in Kiev. We stayed at Ekaterina's house together with two other Russian women. Four of us had to share one big bed and each had to pay Hfl.500 for this 'sleeping place'. In addition, every day one of us was 'on duty': cleaning the house and cooking for the whole family (Ekaterina, her husband and three children) and for the four of us. For this house-work we were not paid. Ekaterina arranged work for us: sometimes cleaning houses, sometimes in the flower business, sometimes in escorting men. We had to pay her 60% of our income. This was real slavery!

Trafficking in women is often linked to trafficking into prostitution. However, this is not completely accurate, since women are also trafficked into other activities, such as domestic work, especially on the "black market." On the other hand, women who choose to work as prostitutes of their own accord, can become the victims of violence and exploitation. The popular approach to trafficking involves deception, violence and fraud, in addition to the illegal transfer of women across borders. But the trafficking discourse is not always useful in regard to prostitution. It would be more correct to refer to forced prostitution as an activity controlled by organized crime (in its different forms) and to voluntary prostitution as a form of business, chosen by the women themselves. During my fieldwork I did not find any evidence of highly organized criminal networks of either Russian or other criminals who were involved in the trafficking of my informants to the West. Neither did I come across information on physical violence against these women or indications that they were forced to work as prostitutes. The highest level of violence I was told about were the threats that were uttered when the costs of a rented apartment were not paid on time.

The argument which was repeated by all my informants was that they came to the Netherlands "to make money," just like "many other women from Eastern Europe do." They were highly motivated by the positive outlook on the economic possibilities voiced by friends who came to the Netherlands before them and were apparently successful in their business. These ideas brought them to the Netherlands even after the prostitution policy changed and they were confronted with a new prostitution law, which had major consequences for both groups, those who already worked in legal sex-clubs and those who planned to join their friends.

The New Dutch Prostitution Law—Past and Present

The changes in the Dutch Brothel Law came into effect on 1 October 2000. The new law offered advantages for sex-workers working in legal brothels and gave prostitution the status of a legitimate profession. It is in fact out of the Dutch concern about trafficking, that the formal legalisation of brothels has come about. Labour laws are supposed to protect the women from exploitation and trafficking and to help them become part of the social security system. But the law contained a paradox: it legitimised prostitution in general, but prohibited prostitutes from outside the European Union to work in legal brothels. Let us examine the background, historical developments and ambiguous character of this unique law. In 2000, when a public and scientific debate on the legalisation of prostitution was launched, it became clear that nothing was new under the sun, most of the arguments pro- and anti- legalisation have their historical precedents, as well as the many attempts by governments to get a grip on prostitution.

Prostitution has always existed and it was tolerated in the Netherlands for long periods (Bossenbroek and Kompagnie 1998; Van de Pol 1996). In Amsterdam, prostitutes were allowed to work in specific areas.[12] The idea was that prostitution, though dishonourable (literally "without honour"), was also indispensable. In the sixteenth century prostitution was prohibited in the North Netherlands after Calvinism was established in 1578, but despite the prohibitive and sometimes repressive measures it was still prospering in the Golden Age of the Dutch Republic. Especially in Amsterdam the prostitution market was flourishing: the city, situated on one of the most important world crossroads was flooded by sailors, traders and women from different Dutch cities or from neighbouring countries, such as Germany and Denmark (Van de Pol 1996; Doornick and Jongedijk 1997).

In 1811, under French rule, brothels were legalised in the Netherlands. The legalisation of brothels led to the registration of prostitutes and better medical supervision. When the French left the Netherlands, there were two types of prostitutes: young women who were registered and medically checked in brothels and women who worked for themselves, outside brothels. The latter category included foreign prostitutes. It was around this time that the international trade in women emerged.

At the end of the ninteenth century prostitution spread into old and new neighbourhoods, no longer in the form of brothels, but in the setting of cafes, bars, cigar-shops, hotels, milk saloons and rented rooms. The brothels disappeared, but prostitutes remained. And prostitution came of age (Bossenbroek and Kompagnie 1998:282). In addition, the influx of prostitutes from abroad never stopped, and once in the Netherlands these women were quickly integrated into the sex-trade business (p.296).

Early in the twentieth century, the conservative Dutch rulers at the time overruled the French regulations by arguing that the citizens of a Protestant society should lead modest and honourable lives. However, the law against brothels was not enforced for many years and attempts to do so were doomed. The main debate in this period was carried out between abolitionists and liberals. The abolitionists promoted arguments of "morality and hygiene" and demanded a total ban on prostitution, while the liberals asked for acceptance and regulation of the profession (Bossenbroek and Kompagnie 1998).

It took almost ninety years before the Dutch Parliament ended the official ban on brothels. The reason: the policy of tolerating existing brothels (the so-called "gedoogbeleid") was deemed hypocritical and organized crime and numerous women traffickers took advantage of this policy. For decades the authorities turned a blind eye to red light districts. In Amsterdam alone there were about 1,000 "window girls," more than 80 sex clubs and about 65 escort agencies in 1999.[13] For generations the Netherlands was internationally well-known for having a tolerant policy toward prostitution in general and migrant prostitution in particular, making it very attractive for sex tourists and other visitors. The role of migrant sex-workers in the Netherlands was important throughout history. In the discourse on trafficking and voluntary prostitution the immigration aspect is sometimes forgotten. In the area of voluntary prostitution anti-immigration issues prevail, the most important of which is the fear of a vast influx of non-EU prostitutes looking for work in Western Europe. In spite of many positive aspects of the new law, one group, perhaps the most numerous and important group of sex-workers was excluded from legal recognition and those who did not have a residence permit were forced to move out of legal prostitution into street prostitution and illegal brothels or to just leave the country.

Voluntary Prostitution and Forced Illegality

In accordance with the new law, Russian-speaking sex-workers without a residence permit were supposed to stop working in legal brothels, if the owner wanted to avoid trouble with the authorities. This did not always happen (see also Goderie et al. 2002) and many non-European prostitutes still work in the same places, but these days they stay out of sight when they sense danger, or they use forged documents. One of my informants, for example, stayed on with her old boss, "as a free-lancer." Many others had no choice but to leave.

Ecstasy

From brothel to independency

Alisa (age 26) worked in a sex-club in Amsterdam until 2001, but after a visit from the police she was asked to leave.

I was sitting in the lobby of a hotel, checking my phone book. I realized I had enough clients to survive at least in the beginning. This was the moment I decided that I would work for myself. I then stayed for a few days in the same hotel before I found an apartment in Amsterdam South and moved in. I told my clients I was now working somewhere else, I did not want them to know that I was working for myself and alone. I also never advertised: all my new contacts went via clients. When a new client arrives, it is usually with a reference from one of my regular clients.

Alisa worked alone, which is quite unusual among Russian-speaking prostitutes. In other cases I found them working in small groups, from 2 to 6 girls. They rent apartments or houses, where they receive their clients, or wait for calls. In one case they worked in an officially registered "alternative medical clinic," owned on paper by a Russian man with a Dutch passport, who played no further role in their activities and during my visits there I never met him personally. In another case two young women received their clients in a small two-room apartment in the centre of Amsterdam. When asked whether the neighbours paid any attention to their activities, they told me that they had never met their neighbours and that "in Holland nobody cares about other people's business." As an example they showed me a newspaper report about an XTC-laboratory in a nearby street that had been in operation for more than two years before it was accidentally discovered by the police.

Strategies of Independency

While illegal Russian-speaking women are working independently in the Netherlands, their resident status makes them vulnerable, at least theoretically, to sexual exploitation, trafficking or forced prostitution. Russian-speaking prostitutes who work for themselves, often have to use various strategies to remain independent. It often happens that they present themselves to their clients as working for certain pimps or in specific brothels, implying that they are not operating on their own. This kind of lying and "identity manipulation" is typical for Russian-speaking prostitutes in the Netherlands. Siegel and Bovenkerk (2001) described Russian call girls in the Netherlands who used an imaginary Russian Mafia threat to chase away local pimps who bullied them (2000:435-437). These are "survival strategies" used by many prostitutes.

Natalia (17) arrived in July 2003 to join her friend Julia (18), who arrived two years earlier. Both work as call girls in Amsterdam.

> *In the beginning we usually went together to different bars to meet, for example, an older man. We would flirt a bit, dance, sometimes drink a glass of vodka, nothing more. Then we said we had to go, and he would leave his business card or telephone number. Then we'd go to another bar and Natalia (her English is better) called him half an hour later and offered to call back if he agreed to her conditions. She used to say we were working for an escort club. Now we don't go 'for the hunt' anymore, we actually almost never go out, just by taxi to clients and back home. There is so much police everywhere! Our neighbours think that we are students at the University of Amsterdam.*

The sophistication of illegal sex-workers, or perhaps more correctly: experienced businesswomen, in the Netherlands is remarkable. Voluntary prostitution is a business and each business has its own ways to survive, to develop and grow. Women who intend to enter this business start to prepare and train long before they arrive in other countries. Unlike the Russian prostitutes who work for criminal groups in the former Soviet Union, whose "training" includes gang rape, the voluntary businesswomen told me about other kinds of qualifications and training: business administration, learning manners and flirting techniques. In the literature on the subject we find more examples of this phenomenon: in Russia, prostitutes were taught by retired, experienced prostitutes, not only how to have sex with their clients, but also how to negotiate a price, just like apprentices in any regular business (Mukhin 2002:55-57).

Though it appeared that illegality did not stop Russian-speaking workers to continue working as prostitutes, they did emphasize some negative aspects, most of which, however, connected to being an illegal alien and not to being a prostitute. Some of them told me that when they needed medical help they had to turn to private doctors, who are sometimes very expensive. They also told me they were often afraid to get caught by the police when they walk around Amsterdam, or drive to clients, or even in the supermarket.

When asked about the competition with legal prostitutes, most of my informants told me that they never tell their clients that they have no legal status in the Netherlands. Instead, they tell them that they work for one or another (nonexistent) club, or for a private pimp. Their clients rarely check their information or ask questions, and "if they do—it will be the last time."

About the competition among illegal sex-workers my informants told me that they try not to have contacts with other "Russians," and those with whom they do, do not know in what kind of business they are involved. They approach their life and work in the Netherlands as a temporary professional business and do not look for wider networks or contacts inside the Russian-speaking community, as other immigrants do (see also Siegel 2002).

Criminal Activities?

As I already emphasized I did not find any clear link between voluntary prostitution and organized crime during my research. In some cases there were attempts by Dutch or other pimps to take advantage of the situation of the prostitutes, especially after they left the brothels. But it seems that the women were able to protect themselves and stay independent. I have heard of only one instance of a 16-year old Russian girl who had to flee from the Netherlands to Belgium, because two Chechen men tried to "convince" her to work for them.

Though I did not find clear evidence of violence or the involvement of criminal organizations, this does not mean that no criminal activities took place. From my conversations with two women I learned about criminal activities, including document forgery, selling fraudulent state identification and social security cards. They bought these documents, in their words, in some "safe places in Amsterdam." It appeared that one woman had contacts with illegal street painters, who "could produce any document you want within an hour." These cases, however, do not prove a link between my informants and any criminal group, either in the Netherlands or in the former Soviet Union.

Conclusion

It appears from my research that the sometimes overly dramatic presentation of the phenomena of prostitution and trafficking is in many cases groundless and exaggerated. Though instances of violence against women in many countries should not be downplayed, it is more and more difficult to make generalizations. As demonstrated in this chapter, there have been new developments in the sex industry in the last years. These developments should be analysed in the context of changing economic and social conditions: the post-reform economic instability and changes in the perception of sex and business in the former Soviet Union on the one hand, and anti-immigration regulations and the Brothel Law in the Netherlands on the other hand.

Voluntary prostitution means freedom of movement, profession and entrepreneurship. Even when forced into illegality, Russian-speaking women still choose to come and stay in the Netherlands because of the economic possibilities and future perspectives. In this context, they view their work in the sex industry as a temporary occupation and an economic necessity and they manage to survive as independent businesswomen.

NOTES

1 EUROPOL, INTERPOL, the Global Survival Network, various NGO's.

2 Among them the film "Ukrexport," a joint production by the U.S. and the EU; documentary films produced by the International Organization for Migration (IOM), etc.

3 Quoted in Hughes (2002:34-35).

4 See also Hughes and Denisova (2001:51).

5 See also Siegel and Yesilgoz (2003).

6 This image, still prevailing in Russia, is perceived differently by the Russian women in the Netherlands. See also further in this article on "Russian wives."

7 To mention some of them: Van Horn, Bullens, Dorelijers, and Jager (2001); NRM (2002); Vanwesenbeek, Hoing and Vennix (2002); Venicz, Nencel, and Visser (2002); Daalder (2002) (all in Dutch).

8 We focused on the economic and cultural links between sex-workers from the former Soviet Union and Turkish clients in Turkey and the Netherlands and on their perceptions of prostitution, masculinity/femininity and sex in general (Siegel and Yesilgoz 2003).

9 Established in 1984, De Rode Draad (the Red Thread) foundation promotes the interests of women employed in the sex industry in the Netherlands by emancipating the business of prostitution through changing the law with a view to improving the rights and working conditions of sex-workers, educating them about their rights and legal obligations and influencing public opinion.

10 In criminological literature the cultural gap is described as a well-known feature of mixed marriages and not typical of Russian-Dutch intermarriages only. The cultural gap is often used as an excuse, or an alibi, for conflicts between the spouses (Hondius 1999; Zaitch 2001).

11 The same pattern is described in Hughes and Denisova (2000:49-51).

12 Pijlsteeg and Halsteeg, and later Haarlemmerdijk and the harbour area.

13 The numbers are not exact, but based on our own calculations during our research on Russian prostitutes and Turkish clients (1999).

REFERENCES

Bossenbroek, M and J.H. Kompagnie. 1998. *Het Mysterie van de Verdwenen Bordelen. Prostitutie in Nederland in de Negentiende Eeuw*. Amsterdam: Uitgeverij Bert Bakker.

Daalder, A. 2002. *Het Bordeel-Verbod Opgeheven. Prostitutie 2000-2001.* Den Haag: WODC.

Doornick, M. and J. Jongedijk. 1997. *In Het Leven: Vier Eeuwen Prostitutie in Nederland.* Apeldoorn: Historische Museum.

Goderie, M., F. Spierings, and S. ter Woerds. 2002. *Illegaliteit, Onvrijwilligheid en Minderjarigheid in de Prostitutie Een Jaar na de Opheffing Van Het Bordeelverbod.* Den Haag: Verwey -Jonker Instituut, WODC, Ministry of Justice.

Hondius, D. 1999. *Gemengde Huwelijken, Gemengde Gevoelens.* Den Haag: Sdu Uitgevers.

Horn. J.E., van, R.A.R. Bullens, Th.A.H. Dorelijers, and M. Jager. 2001. *Aard en Omvang Seksueel Misbruik en Prostitutie Minderjarige Allochtone Jongens.* Amsterdam: VU/Fora.

Hughes, D. 2002. *Trafficking for Sexual Exploitation: The Case of the Russian Federation.* IOM.

Hughes, D. and T. Denisova. 2001. "The Transnational Political Criminal Nexus of Trafficking in Women from Ukraine." *Trends in Organized Crime* 6(3&4):43-68.

Mukhin, A. 2002. *Rossiiskaya Organizovannaya Prestupnost i Vlast: Istoriia Vzaimootnosheniia.* Moscow: Center for Political Information (in Russian).

NRM. 2001. *Mensenhandel, Eerste Rapportage Van de Nationaal Rapporteur.* Den Haag: Bureau NRM.

Pol, L. van de. 1996. *Het Amsterdams Hoerdom. Prostitutie in de Zeventiende en Achttiende Eeuw.* Amsterdam: Wereldbibliotheek.

Siegel, D. 2002. *Russian Biznes in the Netherlands.* Utrecht: Willem Pompe Institute.

Siegel, D. and F. Bovenkerk. 2000. "Crime and Manipulation of Identity Among Russian-Speaking Immigrants in the Netherlands." *Journal of Contemporary Criminal Justice* 16(4):424-444.

Siegel, D. and Y. Yesilgoz. 2003. "Natashas and Turkish Men: New Trends in Women Trafficking and Prostitution." In *Global Organized Crime. Trends and Developments*, edited by D. Siegel, H. van de Bunt, and D. Zaitch eds. Dordrecht: Kluwer Academic Publishers.

Vanwesenbeeck, I., M. Hoing, and P. Vennix. 2002. *De Sociale Positie Van Prostituees in de Gereguleerde Bedrijven, Een Jaar na Wetswijziging.* Utrecht/Den Haag: Rutgers Nisso Groep/WODC.

Venicz, E., L. Nencel, and J. Visser. 2000. *Trends in Prostitutie en Beleid, de Tweede Rapportage van de Profeitstudie*. Amsterdam: Mr. A. de Graafstichting.

Zaitch, D. 2002. *Trafficking Cocaine: Colombian Drug Entrepreneurs in the Netherlands*. Dordrecht: Kluwer Academic Publishers.

Chapter 2

COMMERCIAL SEXUAL EXPLOITATION OF CHILDREN: ASSESSING WHAT WE KNOW AND ITS IMPLICATIONS FOR RESEARCH AND PRACTICE

*Jay Albanese**

- Police raided a house in Plainfield, New Jersey and found four Mexican girls aged 14 to 17, being held against their will and exploited for commercial sexual purposes (Landesman 2004; Mexican Police 2004).
- A Toronto police sweep through "body rub" parlors found five girls under 18 who were engaging in acts of prostitution (Member 2003).
- Four men in Wisconsin were charged as part of a group that performed sex acts with minors and broadcast them live on the Internet (Police 2004).
- Cambodia deported a third American to be tried in the U.S. on charges of sex crimes against Cambodian children, and another U.S. resident was accused of running a child prostitution ring in Cancun, Mexico (Munthit 2004; Granovsky 2004).
- The problem of child sex tourism, where travelers go to foreign countries for illicit sex with minors, has become so serious in Southeast Asia that tourism authorities and other groups are organizing to develop strategies to prevent it (Boediwarhana 2004).

---

* Virginia Commonwealth University and National Institute of Justice, 810 Seventh St., NW, Washington, DC 20531, USA, (justiceworks@yahoo.com).

The points of view expressed are those of the author and do not necessarily reflect the position or policies of the U.S. Department of Justice.

These incidents are a sampling of a growing number of cases reported around the world where children have been exploited for sexual purposes (Broughton 2003; Maeshiro 2003; Man Pleads 2003; Wilson 2003; Halaby 2003; Finger 2003). This chapter aims to better define the problem, what is known about it, how it occurs, and what interventions may hold promise for its reduction and prevention.

What is Commercial Sexual Exploitation of Children?

Commercial sexual exploitation of children (CSEC) encompasses a broad category of related behaviors. A general definition reads:

> The sexual abuse of a minor usually for economic gain; this abuse can take the form of physical abuse, pornography, prostitution, and smuggling of children for unlawful purposes.

In some cases, children have been kidnapped and sold into forced labor in the illegal sex industry. In other instances, impoverished families have sold their children to unscrupulous traffickers in the hope of giving them a better life. There have been documented reports of children held in basements and in slave-like conditions, involving beatings, malnutrition, and continuing threats to them and their families, while they are sexually exploited. More commonly in the United States, children are exploited for sexual purposes by family and friends for monetary reasons. All of these cases conform to the general definition of CSEC above.

A Cycle of Exploitation

A cycle of exploitation often begins when adult family members or friends exploit the trust placed in them and sexually abuse a minor child in their care or custody. This conduct sometimes escalates to systematic sexual behavior involving multiple children, followed by photographed or video-taped sexual abuse that is shared with others via the Internet, or kidnapping and fraudulent abductions of children for purposes of prostitution.

This chapter focuses on child exploitation for commercial purposes, as distinct from individual cases of molestation and sexual abuse where no larger economic motive is present. The criminal justice system has a significant role to play in addressing commercial child sexual exploitation, especially in its more organized forms, because it results in serial victimization of multiple children, involves networks of adult exploiters, and sometimes smuggling, kidnapping, and sale of children as commodities. Individual cases of molestation and sexual abuse are also quite serious and frequently are precursors to commercial child sexual exploitation. Some of the strategies recommended at the end of this publication might be effective in reducing both commercial and non-commercial sexual exploitation of children.

The continuum of abuse is often manifested in the case histories of sexual exploitation victims (see Figure 1). For example, it has been found that victims often come from backgrounds involving abuse, often by a family member. This abuse leads the victim to seek to escape to a better life and to look for love and affection in a better place—making them prime candidates for exploitation by people making promises of a "better life" somewhere else.

Often when the victim comes to the attention of authorities, the public sees her (and sometimes "him") as a teenage prostitute, but this is not an accurate description. Instead, sex is often a means of forced survival for a minor with few visible choices at the hands of an exploitative adult. The term "teenage prostitution" also overlooks the legal status of girls and boys under age 18, who have greater protections under law regarding sexual conduct because of their emotional and physical maturity levels and the need to protect them from exploitive adults. Therefore, it is important that victims of child sexual exploitation are not mistaken for offenders.

What is the Extent of Child Sexual Exploitation?

To date, there has been no concerted effort to obtain reliable, periodic national or regional estimates of the extent of CSEC, against which the size and scope of the problem, and the impact of interventions, can be assessed over time. The largest problem in assessing CSEC, similar to other low-visibility crimes, is the size of the "dark figure." How many cases are not reported?

Nevertheless, some useful information can be gleaned from existing sources. The National Incidence Studies of Missing, Abducted, Runaway, and Thrownaway Children (NISMART) were undertaken pursuant to the Missing Children's Assistance Act, which requires the Office of Juvenile

Continuum of Commercial Sexual Exploitation of Children

(Based on circumstances found in multiple known cases)

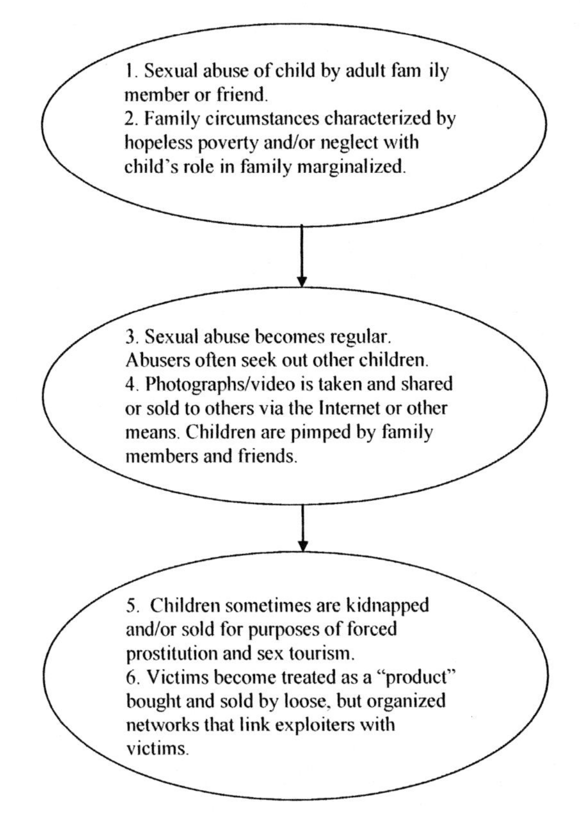

Justice and Delinquency Prevention (OJJDP) to conduct periodic studies on the topic. The most recent NISMART survey involved a representative sample of adults and youth, and found an estimated 58,200 child victims of nonfamily abductions (i.e., friends, acquaintance, and strangers). *Nearly half of all child victims of nonfamily abductions were sexually assaulted by the abductor, and about a third were otherwise physically assaulted.* Most of the victims were ages 12 to 17, and two-thirds were female. Interestingly, 75 percent of the perpetrators were strangers, long-term acquaintances, or friends, as opposed to neighbors, caretakers, other authority figures, or slight acquaintances (Finkelhor, Hammer, and Sedlak 2002). Of course, it cannot be determined from these data what proportion of these children were sexually exploited for commercial purposes, but it is clear that sexual exploitation or physical abuse occurs in the course of most nonfamily abductions of children.

The National Center for Missing and Exploited Children (NCMEC) was established in 1984 as a clearinghouse and resource center to collect and disseminate data regarding missing and exploited children, and it operates a toll-free hotline in the United States. In 1996 the U.S. Congress established the Exploited Child Unit (ECU) within the NECMEC to serve as a resource for issues surrounding the sexual exploitation of children. Beginning in 1998, it established a CyberTipline and website as mandated by Congress for reporting of child sexual exploitation. Reports to the CyberTipLine have risen by 18 times since its first year of existence.

There are several possible reasons why there has been such a dramatic increase in tips regarding child sexual exploitation. They include:

- Growing awareness of the existence of a dedicated resource to call.
- Rapid growth in Internet use worldwide.
- A federal law requiring Internet Service providers to report all incidents of child pornography on their systems to the NCMEC.
- Escalation in the prevalence of sexual exploitation of children and the existence of sexually abusive images of children on the Internet and elsewhere.

Since the CyberTipline was created, more than 200,000 reports have been received of alleged child sexual exploitation. Each verified complaint indicates that at least one child was exploited for sexual purposes.

NCMEC estimates that 1 in 5 girls and 1 in 10 boys are sexually exploited before they reach adulthood, and less than 35 percent of those child sexual assaults are reported to authorities (Missing Kids 2004). Nevertheless, the data that forms the basis for these estimates are incom-

Calls to NCMEC CyberTipline

Year	Tips	Increase
1998	4,578	First year
1999	9,673	111%
2000	19,276	99 %
2001	24,460	27 %
2002	43,097	76 %
2003	81,987	90 %

Source: www.missingkids.com

plete, and the extent of child exploitation for commercial purposes is even less documented.

The true extent of commercial sexual exploitation of children is difficult to determine, but it is important to develop more reliable estimates through research based on known cases, interviews with professionals (e.g., police, victim service providers), and where possible, interviews with victims and offenders. These better estimates will enable more accurate assessment of the size and scope of the problem, trends in its incidence, and a more precise evaluation of the resources being devoted towards intervention, prevention and victim services.

How is Commercial Sexual Exploitation of Children Organized?

There is little reliable information regarding the nature of individuals, networks, and groups involved in the CSEC. Existing data comes from a small number of research studies, reports of nongovernment organizations, and reports to authorities, none of which claims to provide a complete picture of CSEC.

One study combined a nonrepresentative survey of child and youth service providers with interviews of government and nongovernmental organization (NGO) decision makers. It estimated pimps control about 50 percent of street girls engaged in prostitution in the United States (Estes and Weiner 2002). Pimps scout such areas as bus stations, arcades, and malls and focus particularly on girls who appear to be runaways or are lonely and without money or job skills (Klain 1999). At malls, a pimp or his procurer may initiate contact with a girl by offering to buy her something or indicating she could obtain enough money to buy an expensive item if she would be willing to pose for some pictures, which turn out to be pornography and often become a means to blackmail the child into prostitution (Smalley 2003).

Pimps commonly recruit by befriending homeless children, expressing affection, and buying them clothes, jewelry, meals, video games, and the like—with sex taken for granted. Eventually, a child's emotional and financial dependency is used as coercion to sell sex for money, which is turned over to the pimp. In time, the relationship becomes less emotional and more contractual as the pimp sets a minimum on the child's earnings. In one case, a pimp recruited girls mostly in Vancouver, B.C. brought them to Hawaii, and retained their papers so they could not leave. He drugged and handcuffed them, and photographed their sex acts so he could blackmail the girls by threatening to send the photos to magazines or family members (Estes and Weiner 2002:110).

A study in Mexico sought to identify how children are recruited and how exploiters operate and move children from one region to another in six towns: Guadalajara, Acapulco, Cancun, Tapachula, Tijuana, and Ciudad Juarez. This study employed a "snowball" research methodology in which authorities, children, exploiters, and clients identified were interviewed, and in turn, identified other persons for further interviews. The study found that recruitment methods in Mexico appear similar to the United States. In Tijuana, for example, it was reported that girls—generally aged 14 to 17—just arriving in town to find work were recruited under false pretenses by "middlemen or local exploiters," beaten, and threatened that their families would come to harm. Other means of maintaining control over prostituted children include giving them drugs; keeping them in forced isolation by not allowing them to leave their places of work; and trapping them in prostitution through a system of indebtedness that sometimes involves contracts specifying their obligations. In addition to their sexual exploitation in brothels and on the streets, prostituted girls in Mexico—as in other countries—work in hotels, boarding houses, parks, bus stations, bars, night clubs, beauty and massage parlors, modeling and escort agencies, and spas. Adults seeking child sex obtain referrals from waiters, doormen, taxi drivers, receptionists, nightclub security guards, valet parking attendants, and street vendors (Azaola 2001).

Field research based on interviews with pimps and sexually exploited children in several U.S. cities found that most pimps managed one to three girls at any one time and operated along the following lines:

- At least half appear to operate strictly at the local level—neither organized nor part of larger criminal networks.
- At least one quarter may be tied to citywide crime rings, often engaged in drug sales along with prostitution, and appear to be constantly looking for new recruits.
- About 15 percent are reportedly tied to regional or nationwide networks, are well financed and organized, communicate easily with one another (including electronically and via cell phone), often provide support services such as recruitment, selection, indoctrination, and movement of new girls, and occasionally assist in locating and disciplining girls who escaped from other pimps.

- About 10 percent appear to be tied into international sex crime networks and, through them, actively participate in international trafficking of children, including U.S. children. Some pimps are also part of international drug networks and may use children in moving drugs into and across the United States (Estes and Weiner 2002).

Organized crime within and outside the United States can be involved in recruitment and other aspects of sexually exploiting children. Prime targets appear to be those ages 13 and older, often recruited by same-sex peers from among runaway and homeless children, promising financial rewards, nice clothes, a good place to live, and protection. Many adult men and women also recruit children for organized prostitution (Estes and Weiner 2002:110). Figure 2 presents a summary of the types of commercial sexual exploitation of children.

Pedophiles (adults whose primary sexual attraction is to prepubescent children) seek to attract children in ways that are often similar to those used by pimps. Typically, pedophiles offer friendship, food, money, clothing, video games, or a place to shower as a means of luring a child into their homes or cars. Also common are invitations to children to live in the pedophile's apartment, condominium, or house. Sometimes inducements for sex include promises to introduce children to recording or video producers. As noted by the FBI, chat rooms may also provide the pedophile with an anonymous means of identifying and recruiting children (Federal Bureau of Investigation 2003; National Center for Missing and Exploited Children 2003).

A study in Canada focused on pedophiles, and relied on taped conversations the researcher obtained from 19 male subjects between 30 and 50 years old, about half of whom were serving sentences in a Canadian federal prison. It was found that the pedophiles sought vulnerable children through escort agencies and in such locations as arcades, public swimming pools, piercing or tattoo establishments, and shopping centers (Tremblay 2002).

The Intersection of Prostitution with Trafficking and Sex Tourism

It is estimated that about 10 to 15 percent of all homeless and street children in the United States are trafficked for sexual purposes and are caught up in national and international trafficking networks. These children are both U.S. nationals trafficked within and outside the country, as well as children from other countries. Traffickers range from amateurs, to small groups of networked criminals, to those involved in international trafficking operations. According to a White House statement, "Trafficking in persons is often linked to organized crime, and the profits from trafficking enterprises help fuel other illegal activities. The growth of vast transnational criminal networks supported in part by trafficking in persons fosters official corruption and threatens the rule of law" (The White House 2003).

Participants in organized trafficking may include arrangers/investors, who provide money for trafficking operations and oversee the criminal enterprise; recruiters, who are usually based in countries of origin and find migrants and collect fees from them; transporters, who assist moving trafficked persons through origin, transit, and destination countries; corrupt public officials, who receive bribes to provide identity documents and to facilitate exiting and entering countries; informers, who gather information on border surveillance, law enforcement activities, immigration and transit procedures, and the like; debt collectors, who are based in destination countries to collect trafficking fees (which can amount to U.S.$30,000 or more per person); and money movers, who launder trafficking proceeds to disguise their origin. Many foreign children trafficked into the United States work as "sweat-shop" labor under coercive and sometimes slave-like circumstances. These jobs include domestic servants in private homes, cleaning restaurant kitchens, working in laundry rooms of cheap hotels, and factory work (Estes and Weiner 2002:124).

Still others become victims of commercial sexual exploitation. In most cases, one finds a trail of false promises of legitimate work, fraudulent documentation, false destinations, combined in a web of smuggling and intimidation. For example, a trafficked 15-year-old Ukranian girl (interviewed by researchers in Seattle) was transported by private car from a small village to downtown Kiev, by bus to St. Petersburg, by train to Moscow, by plane to Frankfurt, by train to Paris, by plane to Montreal, by cars and vans to the gateway city of Vancouver, by foot across the border into the United States where a private van awaited her. At no time was the girl in possession of a passport or visa identifying her as a person who could enter the United States legally (p.115).

In a report on trafficking, the U.S. Department of State observed that Canada is a destination for persons trafficked into prostitution primarily from China, Thailand, Cambodia, Philippines, Russia, Korea, and

Eastern Europe and a transit point for moving victims from those countries to the United States. Mexico is regarded as a major source and transit point for primarily Mexican and Central American migrants traveling to the United States, some of whom are trafficked for the purpose of commercial sexual exploitation. Others from Asia, South America, and Eastern Europe also transit Mexico into the United States ultimately becoming illegal sweatshop labor or are commercially exploited for sex. The unsuccessful are often forced into prostitution in Mexico, including many children from Central America (U.S. Department of State 2003; Lloyd 2001).

Deception usually plays a core role in traffickers' recruitment efforts: false promises by advertisements, employment agencies, friends, or others often convince families—sometimes through "success" stories—that their children will be safer, better taken care of, and taught a useful skill or trade. Cash may be advanced to families, to be repaid through their child's earnings. Sometimes conditions are stipulated by a "contract," which makes children debt-bonded and provides the leverage needed to force them into prostitution. Traffickers are skilled in providing false documents with false names and ages. Sometimes an easily acquired tourist visa suffices. Traffickers may tell children that if they escape or cooperate with law enforcement, previous cash advances to their families and other money owed will be collected from their parents, who may suffer physical harm (U.S. Department of State 2003:7; Barnitz 2000; The Protection Project 2000).

Child prostitution for sex tourists, which may or may not involve trafficking, is common in selected locations. Sex tourists may include Americans who travel to tourist destinations both within and outside the United States and also international sex tourism businesses either in the United States or abroad. In Tijuana, for example, "Sex tourism is something that happens daily as Americans cross the border every day with the purpose of having a sexual exchange with minors." In Cancun, taxi drivers "recommend places the tourists can go to and receive good commissions for each client" (Azaola 2001:68, 134). Sex tourists usually frequent relatively poor countries that have well-developed commercial sex industries. For example, a U.S. citizen was arrested and convicted in Nicaragua and sentenced to prison for attempting to buy sex from girls between 6 and 12-years old, giving them brand-name clothes and cell phones (U.S. Citizen 2004; Beyer 2001). Sometimes, however, the travel pattern is reversed—from poorer countries (e.g., Argentina, India, and Mexico) to such affluent sex-tourist destinations as Amsterdam, Las Vegas, and New York (Klain 1999).

Pornography

Children are sometimes sexually exploited commercially for purposes of pornography. The producers of child pornography include organized crime, pedophiles, sex tourists, and family members.

- ***Organized crime.*** In contrast to most activity involving child prostitution, organized crime pornographers have been reported to involve children younger than age 9, and sometimes portray them in photos and videos as adults. In a Mexican location, for example, well-organized networks of pornographers have bought girls and boys in poor regions, rotated them from one place to another, and usually kept them under the effect of drugs. In another case, procurers offered parents to give their children (girls and boys ages 6 to 12) an education and a job; parents received monthly payments but did not know that their children were subjects of pornography (Healy 2003; Azola 2001).
- ***Child sex rings.*** Child pornography produced by sex rings is used in members' personal collections and it is frequently offered for publication, sale, or exchange via the Internet or e-mail (Klain, Davies, and Hicks 2001).
- ***Pedophiles.*** Child pornography may play a central role in molestation by pedophiles in justifying their conduct, assisting them in seducing their victims, and blackmailing children to avoid exposure. Some pedophiles have sold homemade videos and photographs of child pornography, with profits occasionally used to help finance trips to sex-tourist destinations (Healy 2003).
- ***Sex tourists.*** Some create pornography as a part of sexual encounters with children. In Tijuana, for example, some Americans are reported to have offered children additional payments if they would let themselves be photographed. In another reported instance, boys were hired as pornography subjects and paid them in cash and drugs. In Acapulco, some reportedly used their houses to keep children under lock and key for days or weeks while producing child pornography. "The children generally agree because, as well as earning some money, during this time they have food, a bed, toys, and, on occasion, drugs" (Azaola 2001:15).

Figure 2. The Organization of Commercial Sexual Exploitation of Children

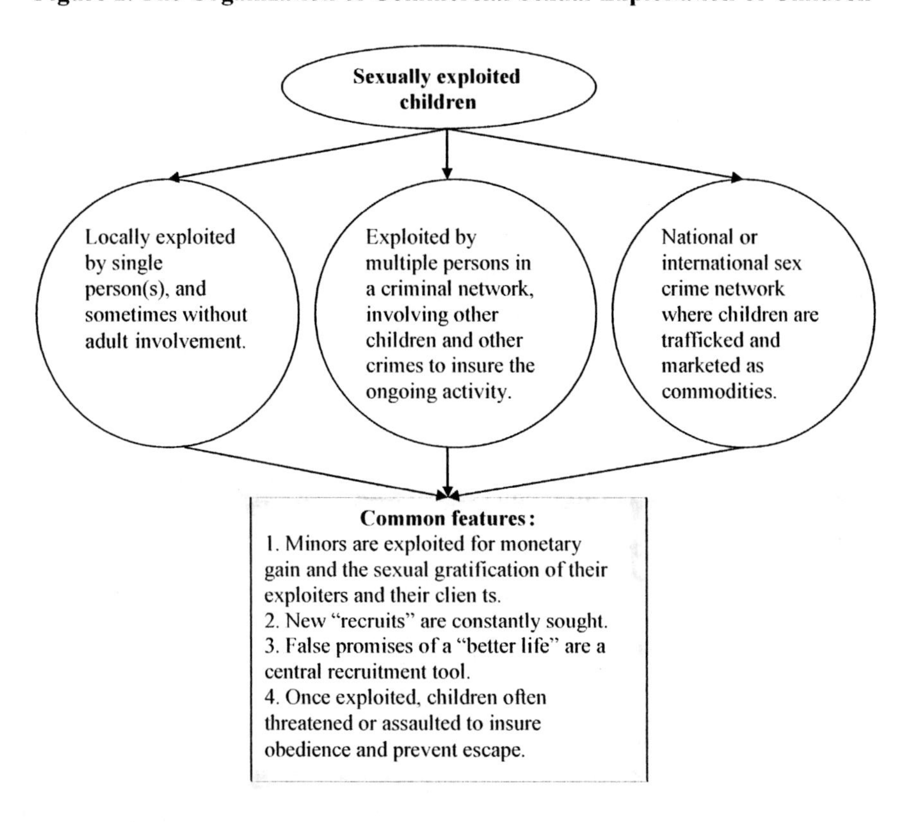

- ***Parents and other family members.*** Children are sometimes photographed by parents as part of intrafamilial child sexual abuse. A U.S.-focused study noted that although child prostitution involves primarily runaways, about 75 percent of child pornography victims lived at home when exploited (Estes and Weiner 2002:151-8). This suggests a significant portion of commercial sexual exploitation of children begins in home settings.

Efforts to Intervene, Reduce, and Prevent Commercial Sexual Exploitation of Children

Efforts to disrupt and prevent the commercial sexual exploitation of children offer hope and direction for the future. These efforts are of three kinds: legislation, developing investigative leads, and multi-agency efforts.

Legislation—Most countries have statutes in place that prohibit sexual exploitation of children, kidnapping, smuggling, and, more recently, trafficking in human beings. These laws usually attach substantial penalties to these crimes. Nevertheless, the globalization of crime, rapid expansion of access to the Internet, and ease of travel have also made it easy for offenders and victims to move effortlessly and disseminate child pornography, while making it difficult to identify the source. Therefore, binding international agreements and treaties are important to address CSEC. Several important international conventions and treaties establish the rights of children and protect them from abduction. The United Nations Convention on the Rights of the Child was enacted in 1990 and is the most widely accepted human rights treaty in the world, designed to improve and living conditions of children globally.

The first World Congress Against Commercial Sexual Exploitation of Children was held in Stockholm in 1996 and was attended by 122 nations, bringing CSEC to light as a world-wide problem. A second World Congress in 2001 attracted three times as many participants and progress was assessed in addressing CSEC. In addition, several multi-lateral treaties have been negotiated on issues of child pornography, sex tourism, and human trafficking (McCoy 2002; Flowers 2001). The United Nations Convention on Transnational Organized Crime has a Protocol to Prevent, Suppress, and Punish Trafficking in persons, especially Women and Children. The purpose of the Protocol is to prevent and combat trafficking, to protect and assist victims, and to promote international cooperation. Protection of victims is a core purpose of the Protocol in recognition of the acute needs of trafficking victims and the importance of victim assistance both as an end in itself and as a means to support the investigation and prosecution of trafficking crimes.

Law enforcement agencies of countries that ratify the Protocol are required to cooperate in the identification of offenders and trafficked persons, share information about the methods of offenders, and train investigators and victim support personnel. Countries are also required to implement security and border controls to detect and prevent trafficking by developing standards for commercial carriers, passports, visas, and other travel documents. In addition to general social prevention measures, the Protocol also calls for measures to prevent re-victimization, where victims who are returned to their countries of origin are sometimes trafficked out again (United Nations Office of Drugs and Crime 2004). The UN Protocol against Trafficking in Human Beings is an enormous international step forward, although some have argued for a separate agreement to address explicitly the abduction of a child for purposes of sex trafficking, child pornography, or prostitution (Higgins-Thornton 2003).

Incentives for Investigative Leads—NCMEC's CyberTipLine has resulted in many apprehensions based on tips from Internet Service Providers (ISP). In one case, an ISP reported to NCMEC's CyberTipline that a particular subscriber had posted images of child pornography to an online group. Using search engines, analysts were able to find identifying information and other evidence left by the suspect on the Internet. Analysts discovered the suspect lived in of Virginia, and public database searches uncovered the suspect's name, address, and social security number. The Bedford County, Virginia, Internet Crimes Against Children (ICAC) Task Force was notified and, the Bedford County Sheriff's Office, working with the FBI, obtained warrants and arrested the suspect. The suspect was charged with nine counts of possession of child pornography as well as manufacturing and distributing child pornography (Missing Kids 2004). The U.S. Office of Juvenile Justice and Delinquency Prevention now funds 40 regional ICAC task forces, which provide expertise to assist in investigations and training involving child sexual exploitation issues (U.S. Senate Judiciary Committee 2003). A publicized tip line, ease of providing Internet tips, training for community groups and law enforcement, and public awareness campaigns through the media help to increase both the likelihood of apprehension for these crimes, as well as public concern. Increasing the perceived obligation to report suspicious activity involving exploited children might be further enhanced through a dedicated reward system for informers in these cases.

Multi-Agency Efforts to Address Multiple Technologies—The Innocent Images National Initiative (IINI) is a component of the FBI's Cyber Crimes Program, a multi-agency investigative effort to combat the proliferation child pornography and child sexual exploitation via computer. The IINI provides coordination and analysis of case information among agencies and governments in order to investigate and prosecute child sexual predators who use the Internet and to establish a law enforcement presence and deterrent on the Internet as an international forum for exchange of information.

From 1996 to 2002, the number of IINI cases opened rose from 113 to 2,370 (Federal Bureau of Investigation 2004). In a similar way, both the U.S. Postal Service and U.S. Customs have programs that focus on child pornography in the mail and children and obscene materials smuggled across borders, respectively (U.S. Customs 2004). Federal cases are prosecuted by the Child Exploitation and Obscenity Section of the U.S. Department of Justice, which also is involved in training and policy development in the areas of child pornography, trafficking, and related crimes (U.S. Department of Justice 2004). This multi-agency response increases the risks for those who manufacture child pornography and traffic children and to customers online, across borders, and via the mails.

Directions for the Future

In addition to current intervention and prevention efforts, there are five directions for the future that can have dramatic impact on the problem of CSEC. These include keeping pace with technology, education of potential victims, public deterrence education, better parental supervision, and the role of women and children in society.

Keeping Pace with Technology—In 2003, the Department of Homeland Security launched a law enforcement initiative known as Operation Predator, aimed at protecting children from pornographers, child prostitution rings, Internet predators and human traffickers. The program is coordinated through the department's Bureau of Immigration and Customs Enforcement (ICE), and it uses the Internet to identify child predators and prosecute them. In partnership with the National Center for Missing and Exploited Children, the program facilitates the exchange of information on missing children who may be involved in these cases. ICE is working with the FBI, the U.S. Postal Inspection Service, the U.S. Secret Service and the Justice Department to develop a National Child Victim Identification Program to provide the nation's first comprehensive program to help police around the world identify and rescue children victimized in the images of child pornography.

The National Child Victim Identification Program has already positively identified exploited children in hundreds of child pornography images. In one case, the New York State Police sent the ICE several child pornography images, and agents were able to positively match five of the images to actual children. The defendant in the case was convicted despite claims that the images were "virtual" or "morphed" images—not actual images of real children (Seper 2003).

The issue of "virtual" versus "actual" images points to the importance of keeping pace with technology. The Child Pornography Prevention Act (CPPA) prohibited possession or distribution of sexually explicit images that appear to depict minors, but are not actual children (18 U.S.C. 2252). This kind of material is produced using computer imaging, or images of adults who appear to be minors. The U.S. Supreme Court held that this law was unconstitutional, because even though the material conveys the impression that minors are depicted, they are not (Ashcroft v. Free Speech Coalition 2002; Markova 2003). However, the Court upheld its earlier decision that child pornography (depicting actual children) is illegal whether or not its meets the legal definition of obscenity, because of the government's interest in protecting the children exploited in producing this material (New York v. Ferber 1982). The Child Online Protection Act (COPA), passed by Congress, was immediately challenged in court for being overbroad in prohibiting any communication for commercial purposes that is available to any minor and that includes any material that is harmful to minors, which includes any, picture, image, graphic image file, article, recording, writing, or other matter that is obscene (18 U.S.C. 231). Problems arose in applying the current U.S. definition of obscenity—which relies on "contemporary community standards"—to the Internet, which is available in places both inside and outside the United States and where community standards differ widely, and also in guaranteeing First Amendment free speech protections to adult information on sex, gynecology, and related issues on the Internet—while protecting children (Ashcroft v. American Civil Liberties Union 2002; Mani 2003; Berg 2000). Congress has been unable, thus far, in striking the balance between regulating the Internet effectively and constitutional protections. It is likely that legislative efforts will continue, however, as concern about offensive material grows in proportion to increases in computer availability and Internet use around the nation and the world.

Education of Potential Victims—Potential victims at risk of exploitation exist both in the United States and abroad. Especially vulnerable are impoverished communities, such as Indian country in the United States, Latin America, and Asia (Echohawk 2001/2002; Mora 2003). Innovative education efforts must be designed to effectively reach the population at risk. Information brochures in regions with very high illiteracy rates, for example, are not likely to be effective. The International Organization for Migration, a nongovernmental organization (NGO), produced an animated short film titled *Shattered Dreams*, designed to raise awareness of youth about the risks of illegal migration. The film is centered on two sisters who decide to go into the big city (Bangkok) for a better life and end up in forced prostitution. The film is also used by social workers providing care for victims of trafficking and exploitation. The film was shown to rescued children in Thailand who had been trafficked to work in factories. Ninety percent said they were not aware of the situation depicted in the film and would not have come to Bangkok had they known the risks (Shattered Dreams 2003). The United Nations Office of Drugs and Crime has produced several public service announcements for television in six languages to raise awareness of trafficking in women and children. The effectiveness of various education efforts needs to be evaluated.

Public Deterrence Education—Commercial sexual exploitation of children remains a demand-driven crime. There is a segment of the population that willingly exploits children and provides a market for child pornography. Deterring these consumers through successful investigations is extremely important, but it is equally important to raise consciousness about the seriousness of the problem, the harm it causes, and the risks of apprehension. The general public needs to become more insistent that resources are devoted to the problem, and they need to be informed about the true nature of the problem of CSEC and the harm it causes to children and families (see Kristof 2004; 2004a). Evidence of such efforts is present in the highly publicized attempts to shut down sex-tour operators in multiple countries (Hanna 2004; Todres 1999). Greater publicity of successful cases and the methods of investigation (e.g., sting operations, undercover agents posing online as children) can further enhance the deterrent impact. Research studies would be helpful in assessing the impact of different approaches to deterrence and education efforts in this area.

Better Parental Supervision—Many CSEC have their origin in absent, negligent, or abusive parenting. The victims of CSEC are indeed children, and it is important to recognize that references to teenage prostitutes, mask the fact that they are child victims of sexual exploitation. As one case study of a teenage girl concluded, the child was not a prostitute, although she engaged in sex for money. "Rather, she was a teenage girl, a child, who, by a series of sad and unfortunate circumstances largely out of her control, found herself to be preyed upon and exploited by at least one very bad man" (Hanna 2002:5). A survey of adult prostitutes at the Atlanta jail revealed that nearly half were molested as children (Hansen 2000). It has been observed that "real cases often involve troubled children who do not meet society's expectations about childhood innocence. Stories of parents prostituting their children for cocaine, and 12-year-olds with 23-year-old boyfriends, are so disturbing that for many people that it is easier to deny the reality of the problem" (Menaire 2001:34; Hansen 2001). Carefully planned and evaluated child abuse prevention programs, more thoughtful and caring treatment of victims, as well as greater attention to abusive households, would help to address important causal circumstances associated with CSEC.

Role of Women and Children in Society—In many places, the role of women and children in society is not valued. They are stereotyped as unworthy of respect, domestic servants, and sex objects. In the words of a judge from the Philippines, these attitudes "are compounded by problems of extreme poverty, massive labor export, globalization, porous borders, aggressive tourism campaigns, negative portrayal of women by mass media, pornography online and Internet chat rooms, the practice of mail-order brides, inter-country adoption, and…visiting foreign military forces" (Vilches 2003:4; Media Institute 2003; Fernando 2001). In the United States as well, many cases of youth prostitution appear to have more to do with decisions regarding survival, rather than sex (Adler 2003; Hansen 2000). In addition, popular culture and music has been criticized for glorifying pimping and treating young women like property (Thompson 2003; Albanese 2005). Research is important to assess and rank the risk factors in the situations of children vulnerable to commercial sexual exploitation, so that both local and global efforts could effectively target their resources to areas shown to be contributing to the problem of CSEC (Wilson 2001).

Conclusion

Commercial sexual exploitation of children produces harm to society at many levels. Efforts have multiplied in recent years to better define the problem, publicize its existence, and develop strategies to reduce its incidence. As technology, communication, and global travel are made easier, efforts to prevent CSEC must improve correspondingly. In addition to existing efforts to improve legislation, enforcement, and cooperative investigations, five directions for the future (keeping pace with technology, education of potential victims, public deterrence education, better parental supervision, and the role of women and children in society) must also be addressed to more effectively prevent commercial child sexual exploitation. Research to assess and rank the risk factors which increase a child's vulnerability to commercial sexual exploitation would be useful in helping to target resources effectively in the global effort to protect children.

REFERENCES

Adler, Libby. 2003. "New Perspectives on Labor and Gender: An Essay on the Production of Youth Prostitution." *Maine Law Review* 55:191.

Albanese, Jay S. 2005. "Looking for a New Approach to an Old Problem: The Future of Obscenity and Pornography." In *Visions for Change: Crime and Justice in the 21st Century*, 4th ed., edited by R. Muraskin and A. Roberts. Princeton: Prentice Hall.

Ashcroft v. American Civil Liberties Union, 122 S. Ct. 1700 (2002).

Ashcroft v. Free Speech Coalition, 535 U.S. 234 (2002).

Azaola, Elena. 2001. *Stolen Childhood: Girl and Boy Victims of Sexual Exploitation in Mexico.* Mexico City: Communicacion Grafica y Representaciones.

Barnitz, Laura A. 2000. *Commercial Sexual Exploitation of Children: Youth Involved in Prostitution, Pornography, and Sex Trafficking.* Washington, D.C.: Youth Advocate Program International.

Berg, Terrence. 2000. "www.wildest.gov: The Impact of the Internet on State Power to Enforce the Law." *Brigham Young University Law Review* 2000:1305.

Beyer, Nancy. 2001. "The Sex Tourism Industry Spread to Costa Rica and Honduras: Are These Countries Doing Enough to Protect Their

Children from Sexual Exploitation?" *The Georgia Journal of International and Comparative Law* 29(Winter):301.

Boediwardhana, Wahyoe. 2004. "ASEAN Tourist Bodies, NGOs Move to Curb Child Exploitation." *Jakarta* Post, January 17.

Broughton, Ashley. 2003. "Men Charged with Felonies in Teen Sex-Video Case," *Salt Lake Tribune,* November 21, p. C8.

EchoHawk, Larry. 2001/2002. "Child Sexual Abuse in Indian Country: Is the Guardian Keeping in Mind the Seventh Generation?" *New York University Journal of Legislation & Public Policy* 5:83.

Estes, Richard J. and Neil Alan Weiner. 2002. "The Commercial Sexual Exploitation of Children in the United States, Canada, and Mexico." February 20. Revised final report submitted to the National Institute of Justice, U.S. Department of Justice.

Federal Bureau of Investigation. 2003. "Online Pornography: Innocent Images Initiative." Retrieved June 9, 2003 (http://www.fbi.gov/hq/cid/cac/innocent.htm).

Fernando, Jude L. 2001. "Children's Rights: Beyond the Impasse." *The Annals of the American Academy of Political and Social Science* 575(May):8.

Finger, Carla. 2003. "Brazil Pledges to Eliminate Sexual Exploitation of Children." *The Lancet* 361(April 5):1196.

Finkelhor, David, Heather Hammer, and Andrea J. Sedlak. 2002. *Nonfamily Abducted Children: National Estimates and Characteristics.* Washington, D.C.: Office of Juvenile Justice and Delinquency Prevention.

Flowers, R. Barri. 2001. "The Sex Trade Industry's Worldwide Exploitation of Children." *The Annals of the American Academy of Political and Social Science* 575(May):147.

Granovsky, Luis. 2004. "Child Prostitution and Sexual Tourism on the Rise in Mexico." *EFE News Service*, February 9.

Halaby, Jamal. 2003. "UNICEF Official Says Children are Victims of Sexual Exploitation and Conflicts." *Associated Press Worldstream,* November 23.

Hanna, Cheryl. 2002. "Somebody's Daughter: The Domestic Trafficking of Girls for the Commercial Sex Industry and the Power of Love." *William and Mart Journal of Women and the Law* 9(Fall):1.

Hansen, Jane O. 2000. "Child Prostitution: Where is Lloydia?." *The Atlanta Journal and Constitutioni,* November 12, p.1A.

_____. 2001. "Prostitutes Getting Younger as Sex trade grows, Judges Say," *The Atlanta Journal and Constitution* January 8, p.A1.

Healy, Margaret A. 2003. "Child Pornography: An International Perspective": 4. Paper serving as a working document for the 1996 World Congress Against the Commercial Sexual Exploitation of Children. Retrieved June 8, 2003 from the Web site of the U.S. Embassy in Stockholm (http://www.usis.usemb.se/children/csec/child pornography.html).

Higgins-Thornton, Shawronda. 2003. "Innocence Snatched: A Call for a Multinational Response to Child Abduction that Facilitates Sexual Exploitation." *Georgia Journal of International and Comparative Law* 31(Spring):619. Retrieved April 7, 2004 (http://www.unodc.org/unodc/en/trafficking_human_beings.html).

Klain Eva J, Heather J. Davies, and Molly A. Hicks. 2001. *Child Pornography: The Criminal Justice System Response*. Washington, DC: National Center for Missing & Exploited Children. March.

Klain, Eva J. 1999. *Prostitution of Children and Child-Sex Tourism: An Analysis of Domestic and International Responses*. Washington, D.C.: National Center for Missing and Exploited Children.

Kristof, Nicholas D. 2004. "Going Home, With Hope," *The New York Times*, January 24.

_____. 2004a. "Bargaining for Freedom." *The New York Times*, January 21.

Landesman, Peter. 2004. "The Girls Next Door," *The New York Times Magazine*, January 25, p.32.

Lloyd, Gregory S. 2001. "Child Sexual Exploitation in Costa Rica," *Indiana International & Comparative Law Review* 12:157.

Maeshiro, Karen. 2003. "Locals Charged in Porn Sweep," *The Daily News of Los Angeles*, November 2.

"Man Pleads Guilty to Sexual Exploitation." 2003. *Associated Press State & Local Wire.* October 24.

Mani, Namita E. 2003. "Judicial Scrutiny of Congressional attempts to Protect Children from the Internet's Harms: Will Internet Filtering Technology Provide the Answer Congress Has Been Looking for?" *Boston University Journal of Science and Technology Law* 9(Winter):201.

Markova, Maria. 2003. “Ashcroft v. Free Speech Coalition: The Constitutionality of Congressional Efforts to Ban Computer-Generated Pornography.” *Whittier Law Review* 24(Summer):985.

McCoy, Amy. 2002. “Children ‘Playing Sex for Money’: A Brief History of the World’s Battle Against Commercial Sexual Exploitation of Children.” *New York Law School Journal of Human Rights* 18(Summer):499.

Media Institute of Southern Africa. 2003. “We Should All Be Ashamed by the Sexual Exploitation of Girls.” *Africa News,* November 25.

“Member of Parliament Calls for Government Talks on Child Sexual Exploitation.” 2003. *Canadian Press Newswire*, December 21.

Menair, Paul. 2001. “Prostitution: Increase Penalties for offenses of Pimping and Pandering of a Minor.” *Georgia State University Law Review* 18(Fall):32.

“Mexican Police Arrest Members of Prostitution Ring with New York Ties.” 2004. *EFE News Services*, February 24.

Missing Kids. 2003. Retrieved February 27 (http://www.missingkids.com/missingkids/servlet/PageServlet?LanguageCountry=en_US&PageId=242).

_____. 2004. Retrieved April 7 (http://www.missingkids.com/missingkids/servlet/PageServlet?LanguageCountry=en_US&PageId=376).

Mora, Jose Eduardo. 2003. “Rights-Central America: Poverty Spurs Growth of Child Sex Rings.” *Inter Press Service*, October 14.

Munthit, Ker. 2004. “American Accused of Child Sexual Abuse Sent to U.S.,” *Associated Press Worldstream*, February 17.

National Center for Missing & Exploited Children. 2003. “Internet-Related Exploitation Background,” Washington, D.C.: National Center for Missing & Exploited Children: 1. Retrieved May 22, 2003 (http://www.missingkids.org/missingkids/servlet/PageServlet?LanguageCountry=en_US&PageId=1213).

New York v. Ferber, 458 U.S. 747 (1982).

“Police Say Ring Victimized Wisconsin Children.” 2004. *The Associated Press State & Local Wire*, January 29.

Seper, Jerry. 2003. “Initiative Targets Child Exploitation.” *The Washington Times*, July 10.

"'Shattered Dreams' to Educate Migrants." 2003. *The Nation (Thailand)*, November 12. Retrieved April 7, 2004 (http://www.iom.int/en/news/pbn031003.shtml#item4).

Smalley, Suzanne. 2003. "This Could Be Your Kid," *Newsweek*, August 18.

The Protection Project. 2000. *Trafficking in Persons, Especially Women and Children in the Countries of the Americas*. Washington, D.C.: Johns Hopkins University School of Advanced International Studies.

The White House. 2003. "Fact Sheet: Trafficking in Persons National Security Presidential Directive," February 25. Retrieved May 22, 2003 (http://usinfo.state.gov/topical/global/traffic/03022502.htm).

Thompson, Carla. 2003. "Hottest Hip Hop Glorifies Pimping." *Inter Press Service*, November 11.

Todres, Jonathan. 1999. "Prosecuting Sex Tour Operators in U.S. Courts in an Effort to Reduce the Sexual Exploitation of Children." *The Boston Public Interest Law Journal* 9(Fall):1.

Tremblay, Pierre. 2002. "Social Interactions Among Pedophiles": 10–17. Paper based on a study funded by the Canadian Ministry of Justice and sponsored by the International Bureau for Children's Rights (Montreal), May.

"U.S. Citizen Convicted in Child Sex Case in Nicaragua." 2004. *EFE News Services*, March 2.

U.S. Customs. 2004. Retrieved April 7 (http://www.customs.ustreas.gov/xp/cgov/enforcement/ice/investigative_priorities/; http://www.usps.com/postalinspectors/prohmenu.htm).

U.S. Department of Justice. 2004. Retrieved February 19 (www.usdoj.gov/criminal/ceos/mission.htm).

U.S. Department of State. 2003. *Trafficking in Persons Report June 200.* Washington, D.C.: U.S. Department of State.

U.S. Senate Judiciary Committee. 2003. "Pornography Victim Protection." Testimony of J. Robert Flores, Administrator, Office of Juvenile Justice and Delinquency Prevention, Office of Justice Programs. October 15.

United Nations Office of Drugs and Crime. 2004. "Trafficking in Human Beings." Retrieved April 7, 2004 (http://www.unodc.org/unodc/en/trafficking_human_beings.html).

Vilches, Judge Nimfa Cuesta. 2003. "Commentary: Trafficking of Women and Children." *Businessworld*, December 17, p.4.

Wilson, Patrick. 2003. "Man Arrested on Charges Involving Sexual Photos." *Winston-Salem Journal*, December 19, p. B1.

Wilson, Robin Fretwell. 2001."Children at Risk: The Sexual Exploitation of Female Children After Divorce." *Cornell Law Review* 86 (January):251.

Chapter 3

INTELLECTUAL PROPERTY THEFT, ORGANIZED CRIME, AND TERRORISM

*Hedieh Nasheri**

Intellectual property violations have grown in both magnitude and complexity. Traditionally, intellectual property crimes, terrorism, and organized crime activities have been considered separately, much as drug trafficking, organized crime, and terrorism were considered until recently. Now, law enforcement and the intelligence community have been telling us that a growing concern is the convergence of different types of illicit activities in order to further the goals of clandestine activities and operations (Hearing of the House International Relations Committee 2003). Intellectual property theft, including selling counterfeit software and hardware, is supporting more serious crimes such as drug trafficking and terrorism according to a recent study conducted by the Alliance Against Counterfeiting and Piracy in the U.K. (Alliance Against Counterfeiting and Piracy 2003:7).[1]

As worldwide dependence on technology increases, high-tech crime is becoming an increasingly attractive source of revenue for organized crime and terrorist groups, as well as an attractive option for them to make commercial and financial transactions that support criminal activity. Criminal activity in the cyber world presents a daunting challenge at all

* Department of Justice Studies, 113 Bowman Hall, Kent State University, Kent, Ohio, 44242, USA, (hnasheri@kent.edu).

This chapter developed as part of a larger study addressing the global scope of intellectual property law which is currently being conducted for the International Center at the National Institute of Justice as part its efforts on developing a transnational crime agenda.

levels of law enforcement. In the past, a nation's border acted as a barrier to the development of many criminal enterprises, organizations, and conspiracies. Over the past decade, the advent of the Internet as a business and communication tool has erased these borders. Cyber criminals and organizations pose significant threats to global commerce and society (Nasheri 2004).[2]

What is the Link between Intellectual Property Crimes, Organized Crime Groups and Terrorism?

Investigation conducted by the International Chamber of Commerce shows that organized criminal groups are involved in trademark counterfeiting and copyright piracy (Hutchinson 2003). The European Commission, Interpol, and many enforcement authorities, from the U.K. to Australia, have accepted that "piracy and organized crime go hand in hand" (Valenti 2003:5). For example, numerous U.S. government agencies are highlighting the link between organized crime and copyright piracy (United States Department of Treasury 2001).[3] According to the Federal Bureau of Investigation's website available at http://www.fbi.gov/hq/cid/fc/fifu/about/about_ipc.htm:

> There is also strong evidence that organized criminal groups have moved into IP crime and that they are using the profits generated from these crimes to facilitate other illegal activities. There are a number of reasons for the dramatic increase in IP crime in recent years. First, many forms of IP can be produced with minimal start-up costs making IP crimes accessible to large numbers of people; second, international enforcement of IP law is virtually nonexistent; and finally, domestic enforcement of IP laws has been inadequate and consequently the level of deterrence has been inadequate.

Law enforcement officials from the United States and abroad are exploring a striking new theory that terrorist organizations, including Al-Qaeda, Hamas, and Hezbollah, are using the profits from the increasingly organized trade in counterfeit merchandise to fund their operations. There is evidence that terrorist groups are becoming more creative with respect to financing their operations, partly due to the United States government's increased pressures against traditional terrorist fundraising schemes and the terrorist groups' desire to operate in an arena where profits are high and penalties are low (Hyde 2003). Conseqently, fighting counterfeiting has become part of the counter-terrorism campaign.

The Nature of Terrorist Financing

Prior to 1991, almost all active terrorist groups relied in some measure on countries to bankroll their activities (e.g., the Soviet Union, Iran, Iraq, Libya, Syria, Saudi Arabia, Greece, and Cuba). But the collapse of the Soviet empire in 1991 cut off an important source of funds to many terrorist groups, especially communist groups. Moreover, states that had funded and protected terrorist groups began reducing their support due to international pressure. Libya, for example, dramatically scaled back its support for terrorist groups following United Nations sanctions levied against it for its role in the bombing of Pan Am Flight 103. Consequently, terrorist groups turned to a variety of activities, including charitable contributions, narcotics trafficking, cigarette smuggling and selling counterfeit products (Johnson 2003).

Terrorist groups are behaving much like international crime syndicates, developing increasingly sophisticated financial infrastructures to generate dependable revenue sources (Lantos 2003). Organized crime figures and terrorists are sophisticated in that they share information and they investigate for high profit endeavors that are low priorities for the police, where they can engage in their activity and make a profit without the fear of significant investigation resulting in arrests. For example, Operation Green Quest was a multi-agency task force established by the United States Treasury Department, aimed at identifying, disrupting and dismantling the terrorist financial infrastructure and sources of funding—this operation specifically recognized counterfeit merchandise schemes as a source of terrorist funding (United States Department of Treasury 2001).

Terrorist organizations worldwide are looking for a variety of illegal activities to fund their efforts and therefore seek diverse income streams. Terrorist financing is the generation of funds via illicit means that are then remitted to a terrorist organization or its front organization via formal or informal financial channels. These funds may be used for either the operating costs of the organization or to carry out terrorist activities and attacks. These organizations have looked at drug trafficking, contraband, counterfeiting and piracy, as means of illegal activity to fund their organizations. As the United States and its allies work to shut down terrorist groups funding networks and money laundering schemes, it is likely that Al-Qaeda and other groups will increase their focus on intellectual property crimes as a way of obtaining funds (Hearing of the House International Relations Committee 2003).

The links between intellectual property crime and terrorist financing can be categorized in the following manner:

Direct Involvement

Direct involvement is evident where the relevant terrorist group is implicated in the production, distribution or sale of counterfeit goods and remits a significant portion of those funds for the activities of the group. Terrorist organizations with direct involvement include groups who resemble or behave more like organized criminal groups than traditional terrorist organizations. An example of this is the case of Northern Ireland where paramilitary groups have engaged in criminal activities including intellectual property crime. These criminal activities range from control or investment in manufacturing or fabrication to taxing the market stalls where counterfeit goods are sold (Millar 2002; Sommerlad 2000).[4]

Indirect Involvement

Indirect involvement is evident where sympathizers or militants are involved in intellectual property crime and remit some of the funds, knowingly to the terrorist groups they sympathize with. In many cases the funding is further attenuated, involving unrecorded movements of cash via third parties. This seems to be the case with some groups like Hezbollah and the Salafi Group for Call and Combat (Von Radowitz 2002).[5]

Specific Examples

A growing body of evidence indicates that terrorist organizations are already involved in and profiting from large scale counterfeiting and piracy. The following examples, compiled from public source news articles and government reports, establishes the existence of genuine connections between counterfeiting/piracy and terrorism.

Federal authorities in the United States have several investigations under way examining evidence suggesting that Hezbollah, Hamas, and other terror networks might be selling counterfeit products to pay for their worldwide activities. The FBI, Customs Service, and other agencies are investigating the sale of stolen or counterfeit computer software, t-shirts and handbags (Mintz and Farah 2002).[6] Furthermore, according to some media reports, the FBI had compiled strong evidence that the 1993 terrorists in New York City financed their activities with counterfeit textile sales from a store on Broadway (Nurton 2002; Stern 1996).[7] And, the Basque terrorist group (ETA) in Spain is involved in the sale of counterfeit clothes and handbags (Von Radowitz 2002).

Mohamod Hammoud

In February 2003, federal prosecutors in Brooklyn, New York charged six men with importing up to 35 million counterfeit cigarettes from China into the United States. The men were accused of importing the fake cigarettes, then selling them through a tax free business located at an upstate New York Indian reservation and also through a website (http://www.smoke cheap.com). The cigarettes were allegedly imported into the United States in 5 separate shipments through New Jersey ports over a two year period. The charging documents stated that the counterfeiters hid the cigarettes in shipping containers behind kitchen pots. According to the prosecutors, the men were also under investigation in Europe for cigarette smuggling. Two of the defendants were also charged with importing counterfeit batteries from China via Lithuania (Glaberson 2003; Marzulli 2003). In June 2002, Hammoud was convicted of providing aid to a terrorist organization. The indictment papers surrounding the case stated that Hezbollah officials in Lebanon asked cell members to purchase equipment such as "computers, night vision equipment, mine-detection devices, global-positioning devices, and advanced aircraft-analysis software" (Goldberg 2002:74).[9] On February 28, 2003, Mohamad Hammoud was sentenced to 155 years in prison for helping to lead a cigarette smuggling operation out of North Carolina that funneled money to Hezbollah. The Hezbollah cell operated out of Charlotte, North Carolina, and over the course of a year and a half sold close to $8 million worth of smuggled cigarettes in Michigan. Ten members of the smuggling ring were arrested and eight members pled guilty.

Dubai, Copenhagen, and Denmark

In the recent past there has also been media accounts reporting a link between Al-Qaeda and the trafficking of counterfeit goods. Recovered Al-Qaeda terrorist training manuals revealed that the organization recommends the sale of fake goods as one means to raise funds to support terrorist operations (Von Radowitz 2002).[9] An investigation into a shipment of fake goods from Dubai to Copenhagen and other areas of Denmark suggested that Al-Qaeda itself may be funding itself by trafficking in counterfeit goods. Danish Customs, using sophisticated risk analysis software, examined one of the containers on board and discovered that it contained over one thousand crates full of counterfeit shampoos, creams, cologne, and perfume. The goods were ultimately bound for the United Kingdom. The United Kingdom later revealed that the sender of the counterfeit goods was a member of Al-Qaeda. This connection was later confirmed by the European Commission's Customs Coordination Office. The intelligence services of three countries—Denmark, the United Kingdom and the United States—were involved in investigating the matter (Taylor 2003).

It is difficult to determine whether the funds from this traffic went directly to Al-Qaeda or whether only a part of them were remitted. In general, it is possible that funds generated through intellectual property crime are remitted to Al-Qaeda indirectly through zakat-based giving (a religious duty to give money). Given the cash-based nature of this giving it is difficult to establish the provenance of the funds.

Paraguay and the Triple Frontier Region

Counterfeit operations in Paraguay's tri-border region where the countries of Brazil, Argentina, and Paraguay meet have also been used to raise money to support terrorist operations and groups (Millar 2002; Rother 2002; Junger 2002). For nearly three decades, the Triple Frontier has served as a friendly operations center for international "smugglers, counterfeiters and tax dodgers" and has earned a reputation for being one of the most lawless places on the planet (Goldberg 2002; Rother 2002). Inhabitants of and visitors to the region move with relative ease among the three countries as they attempt to evade what little official authority exists in the region. Despite repeated and persistent industry complaints, counterfeit and pirate products saturate the region, especially in the Paraguayan border-town of Ciudad del

Este. For years, the United States Trade Representative (USTR) has routinely subjected Paraguay to Section 306 Monitoring in its annual "Special 301" reports and cited the government for unacceptably high levels of intellectual property theft.[10] Further evidence demonstrates the tri-border area as a regional hub for Hezbollah and Hamas fundraising activities (Millar 2002; Rother 2002; Junger, 2002).[11]

One important fund raising figure for Hezbollah, who once inhabited the Triple Frontier region and is now a fugitive, is a man by the name of Ali Khalil Mehri. Paraguayan authorities and American industry representatives considered Mehri to be one of the leading distributors of pirate CDs. In its 2000 *Patterns of Global Terrorism Report*, the United States Department of State noted that Paraguayan authorities arrested Mehri for violating intellectual property laws and for aiding an enterprise that was distributing copies of CDs that espoused Hezbollah's extremist ideals. A Paraguayan terrorist task force raided Mehri's apartment and found guns and pirate discs. Faulty judicial procedures, however, allowed for his release and he soon fled back to Lebanon (Goldberg 2002; United States Department of State 2000; Global Options, Inc. and Reconnaissance International Report 2003).[12]

One specific example detailing the link between counterfeiting and terrorism deserves a greater degree of attention. A Congressional delegation led by the Western Hemisphere Subcommittee Chairman, Cass Ballenger, traveled to the tri-border area to meet with the local law enforcement officials. It was during this trip that the delegation members and staff viewed warehouses full of confiscated counterfeit American items. According to the delegation one of the most disturbing items was a counterfeit Microsoft CD-ROM flight simulation program that was being marketed by depicting the September 11th attack with Osama Bin Laden on the front cover of the CD (Hearing of the House International Relations Committee 2003). The delegation learned that this item and numerous others were confiscated in raids of businesses owned by individuals with established links to Hezbollah and Hamas. Among items confiscated were also propaganda supporting terrorism.

Lebanon

In another account, in October 2001 a joint initiative led by the United States Immigration and Customs Enforcement and the Federal Bureau of

Investigation received several referrals from JFK Airport Customs inspectors concerning a pattern of intellectual property seizures from Lebanese manufacturers. This investigation resulted in 15 seizures over a four-month period. According to intelligence sources, the Lebanese importers based in New York City and Detroit were using counterfeit importations as a means of funding terrorist organizations, such as Hezbollah (Hearing of the House International Relations Committee 2003).

Northern Ireland

In Northern Ireland the counterfeit product market is estimated to cost the economy in excess of $167 million. In 2002, the police seized in excess of $11 million in counterfeit products. It is known that paramilitary groups are involved in intellectual property crime, including counterfeit cigarette trafficking. Paramilitary involvement in intellectual property crimes in Northern Ireland is conducted through their control of the markets where many counterfeit goods are sold. Other aspects of intellectual property crimes in Northern Ireland appear to have no terrorist involvement (i.e., the importation and sale of counterfeit clothing which is dominated by individuals in the South Asian community in Northern Ireland) (Millar 2002; Sommerlad 2000).[13]

Kosovo

A significant portion of consumer goods available for sale in Kosovo, such as CDs, DVDs, clothes, shoes, cigarettes, and computer software, are counterfeit. The sale of counterfeit goods occurs openly and there is limited enforcement against counterfeit products due to significant legal loopholes.

There is a long-standing relationship in Kosovo between criminal organizations and local ethnic-Albanian extremist groups. This relationship is based on family or social ties. It is suspected that funds generated from intellectual property crimes benefit both criminal organizations and extremist groups (Hearing of the House International Relations Committee 2003).

Organized Criminal Activity and Piracy

Both the production and distribution of high quality counterfeit software require a high level of planning, funding, and organization; and access to replicating equipment, raw materials, packaging, shipping facilities, and money laundering avenues. Because of the enormous opportunities for profits and the low risk of prosecution or significant punishment, software counterfeiting has become part of an intricate web of international organized crime. Highly organized criminal syndicates frequently have significant resources to devote to their illegal operations, thus increasing the scope and sophistication of their criminal activity. Furthermore, by nature, these syndicates control international distribution channels which allow them to move massive quantities of pirated goods, as well as other illicit goods, throughout the world. An emerging concern is the fact that traditional organized crime syndicates appear to be playing a dominant role in the production and distribution of certain types of hard goods piracy, such as optical disks.

The following examples are clear instances of organized criminal groups who engage in trafficking of counterfeit goods.

Asia

Throughout Asia, organized crime groups operate assembly lines and factories that generate literally millions of pirated optical discs. These groups pirate a full range of products ranging from music to software to movies to video games. Anything that can be reproduced onto an optical disk and sold around the globe is available. There is also anecdotal evidence that syndicates are moving their production operations onto boats sitting in international waters to avoid law enforcement (Malcolm 2003). Industry representatives in Asia report that they have been threatened and their property has been vandalized by members of organized crime syndicates when their anti-piracy efforts strike too near the illegal operation. Government officials have also been threatened (Malcolm 2003). Additionally, many organized piracy groups from Asia use South America, most notably Paraguay, as a transshipment point for pirated products.

Britain

In April 2000, as a result of an investigation by the British authorities into the supply of high quality counterfeit CDs linked forensically to Russian plants, a series of raids were conducted in London and four persons were arrested. During the search, a sophisticated credit card counterfeiting operation was uncovered. The suspects, Russian nationals who had been granted political asylum in Britain, employed members of the Russian community in London, to secretly record details of credit cards when these were tendered for payment in restaurants and hotels. The data obtained was then downloaded onto computers and subsequently written to blank cards, which were used to purchase high value items from London stores. Forensic examination of the computers revealed that over 30,000 credit card details were recorded. At the suspects' addresses, 10,000 blank credit cards were found together with stamps for attaching holograms and machinery for printing and embossing the cards. The sale of CDs financed the credit card operation with a network of couriers smuggling the discs into the U.K. (Grant 2003).

Italy

In February 2003, the Italian Mafia boss, Luigi Giuliano, described in a trial the role of organized crime in music and video piracy. Giuliano, La Forcella (Naples downtown) Camorra boss, arrested in 2001, turned State's evidence and provided information on organized crime activities and strategies in Naples in the last two decades.

On February 5, 2003, in front of the Public Prosecutor Filippo Beatrice, Giuliano stated that the Camorra clans earn some "100,000 Euros each week dealing with drugs, extortion and video and music piracy." He described in detail how organized crime manages all the illegal operations in Naples, with different gangs controlling the calls for tenders, the drugs sales, the illegal betting, and the production of counterfeit CDs in different city areas. These "local" gangs keep part of the illegal incomes while other monies are deposited in the Camorra bosses' bank accounts. Giuliano confirmed that the Camorra gang was directly involved in the production and distribution of pirate CDs, not just controlling the area used by organized crime to run illegal activities. Giuliano told the judges that in the early 1980s, during a major war between the various gangs in which dozens were killed, the "Cupola," the illegal main board of the criminal alliance, agreed on the distribution of the illegal activities to various gangs. The "pax mafiosa" which followed the agreement allowed the criminal network to increase the business in many areas including the emerging piracy business (Grant 2003).

Malaysia

An attorney from the Computer Crime and Intellectual Property Section (CCIPS) of the United States Department of Justice visited Kuala Lumpur in 2003 to conduct law enforcement training for Malaysian prosecutors and agents. According to Malaysian officials with whom he spoke, many, if not most, of the optical disk production facilities in Malaysia are owned and operated by organized crime syndicates, specifically very wealthy and powerful criminal gangs from Taiwan that control a significant number of facilities not just in Malaysia but across Asia generally (Malcolm 2003).

The reach of organized crime appears to extend beyond the production of optical disks into the distribution chain. While in Malaysia, that same CCIPS attorney visited an open air market, similar to ones found in large cities around the world, which offered a myriad of pirated products. While touring the market, the attorney learned that many vendors offer their goods on tables covered in brightly colored cloths which indicates the vendor's affiliation with a specific criminal syndicate. One vendor may use a red cloth to show his affiliation with one criminal gang, while his neighbor offers his wares on a blue cloth signifying his affiliation with another criminal gang (Malcolm 2003).

Mexico

In October 2001, Mexico Police raided eleven houses, three of which were linked by interconnecting passages and tunnels, which were disguised by false walls. Inside they discovered a massive counterfeiting operation. In total, five persons were arrested during searches, which yielded 235 CDR burners, over 1 million blank CDRs and 512,000 pirated CDRs together with over 1,000,000 inlay cards. This illegal plant had the potential capacity to produce over 14 million CDRs annually. It is believed that this crime syndicate invested the profits from piracy into other activities such as narcotics and prostitution (Grant 2003).

In July 2002, an investigation led to a Mexican police raid that was met with fierce resistance from five juveniles aged under 18. There were 5kg of cocaine in the premises along with 25 CDR burners and 16,000 pirate CDRs. Using juveniles to run CDR and drug trafficking operations is a deliberate ploy by organized crime to protect those behind the syndicate (Grant 2003).

Spain

In January 2003, a series of 13 raids by the National Police in Madrid led to the arrest of 40 persons involved in the mass duplication of CDRs. The suspects, many of whom were illegal immigrants from China and who had been brought to Spain by the other members of the gang, were found in possession of 346 high speed burners, 168,400 blank CDRs, 24,450 recorded CDs, 39,000 DVDs, 10,500 VCDs with films, 515,000 jewel cases, 210,000 inserts and 48,000 Euros in cash. The gang used a number of computer shops and restaurants to launder the money generated by the pirated product (Grant 2003).

Taiwan

In May 2001, a raid on residential premises in Kaoshung City revealed 70,000 suspected pirate discs. Most contained pornographic material but more significantly the search of the premises revealed several illegal firearms. These guns were Italian and German self-loading pistols. Five persons were arrested. As a result of these arrests, further searches were carried out and small quantities of pirate product and further firearms seized. At a third premises an illegal arms factory was discovered running alongside a sophisticated CDR facility. In total, 17 rifle barrels, 7 modified handgun barrels, 10 shotgun barrels, 10 cartridge magazines, 50 bullets and other equipment were seized. The main suspect in this case had previous involvement in music piracy (Grant 2003). Industry groups have reported that organized crime from Taiwan and other parts of the world control much of the distribution of optical disks into Latin America through Ciudad del Este (Llorito 2003a; Llorito 2003b).

National Examples of Piracy and Counterfeiting Rings

It is also true that the pirated goods produced by organized crime syndicates enter into and are distributed throughout the United States. There is ample evidence, for example, that Taiwanese triad members import massive amounts of counterfeit software and other counterfeit products, such as trademarked computer chips into the United States. The reach of these organized crime operations is undeniably global in scope (Malcolm 2003).

Chinese Organized Crime Syndicate

Organized crime from New York to Los Angeles has been suspected of intellectual property theft. Law enforcement officials in L.A. investigated the involvement of the Wah Ching Chinese organized crime syndicate in a counterfeit software ring. A recent raid of that syndicate netted $10.5 million in counterfeit Microsoft software, shotguns, handguns, TNT, and plastic explosives. Ultimately, three Asian organized crime groups were believed to be involved (International Anti-Counterfeiting Coalition 2003).

Counterfeit Handbag Shop in New York

A raid of a souvenir shop in mid-town Manhattan led to the seizure of a suitcase full of counterfeit watches and the discovery of flight manuals for Boeing 767s, some containing handwritten notes in Arabic. A similar raid of a counterfeit handbag shop in New York in 2002 uncovered faxes relating to the purchase of bridge inspection equipment. Two weeks after the raid of the handbag shop, police in New Jersey were investigating an assault on a Lebanese member of an organized crime syndicate. During a search of the man's apartment, authorities found fake drivers' licenses and lists of suspected Al-Qaeda terrorists—including the names of some workers from the handbag shop that had been raided (Nurton 2002).

Threats and Responses

The above cases demonstrate the critical need for close cooperation between nations and international law enforcement. How can we successfully fight a well-financed global network of piracy and counterfeiting rings, when the criminals who control these operations bear little risk of prosecution and meaningful punishment outside of the United States?

Based on the above accounts of intellectual property crime activities, it is reasonable to make the following assessments:

- Intellectual property crime is global in its scale and scope, generating significant amounts of illicit profit for criminal groups,
- The high volume of counterfeit and pirated products found in the global market indicates that the illegal industry has graduated from

"mom and pop" operations and the profits from counterfeiting and piracy are so high that they attract all types of organizations to this activity (Trainer 2003),

- Intellectual property crime is a low risk/high return activity, due to the low penalties if caught, and the high return in relation to the initial investment,
- Intellectual property crime now seems to be dominated by criminal organizations,
- Most terrorist and organized crime groups do not take responsibility for the development and control of counterfeit production and distribution; rather they benefit indirectly from funds remitted to them from sympathizers and militants involved in intellectual property crime, and
- It is possible that intellectual property theft is likely to become a more important source of financing for terrorist groups because it is low risk/high return.

In today's global and technologically advanced marketplace counterfeiters can no longer be dismissed as simple con-artists or isolated street peddlers trying to earn a few extra dollars. The reality is that counterfeiters and pirates steal from corporations, steal from the community, steal from the government, steal from the consumers they deceive and pose real dangers to the public health and safety. It is no secret that highly sophisticated and organized criminal syndicates exert significant influence and control over the manufacturing, distribution and sale of counterfeit and pirated goods.

Independent consultants calculate that the global music piracy market has cost the music industry between $4 billion and $5 billion per annum. Alarmingly, unlike the legitimate market, it is a growth industry fueled in part by advances in technology. As previously mentioned, however, it is the proliferation of organized crime group involvement which gives rise to the greatest concern. Evidence suggests that organized crime is firmly entrenched in music piracy, and it would be surprising, given the potential profits, if they were not involved in other piracy (Hearing of the House International Relations Committee 2003).

In sum, organized crime and terrorist groups tend to turn their hand to diverse areas of criminal activity, motivated primarily by profit, therefore the surfacing of a nexus between intellectual property theft and offenses such as drug trafficking, fraud, illegal firearms and terrorism is not uncommon. In light of the links, governments around the world cannot afford to allow such activities to remain unchecked. The threat is real and considerable, as evidenced by the examples provided in this chapter, and the response must be coordinated to be effective.

What Steps Needs To Be Taken

Developing more and better intelligence about organized crime and terrorist groups and their operations is just the first step in what will be a long and potentially difficult process of targeting this type of activity. Because most of these syndicates operate outside the United States, the United States must rely on foreign governments for much of the enforcement efforts in this area. More cooperation among law enforcement globally is necessary. If a government lacks the will or the expertise to enforce IP laws, organized crime will continue to proliferate with impunity. Even in countries that have the will and expertise to fight back, a lack of investigative resources, inadequate laws, a judicial system that will not impose serious sentences, or corruption can grind IP enforcement to a halt (Malcolm 2003).

Clearly, we cannot succeed until all governments recognize that intellectual property crime is a serious crime that demands the same level of enforcement and cooperation that other global organized crime activities receive. It is a necessity that law enforcement agencies join together in sending a clear, unified, and unequivocal message to the international authorities that intellectual property crime is a major priority that demands tough penalties and multilateral cooperation among nations and with private companies. Increasing criminal statutes for product counterfeiting and increased awareness among the general public is required to recognize what happens to the money when the consumer gets that "great bargain" on the street.

NOTES

1 According to a study conducted by the Alliance Against Counterfeiting and Piracy (AACP), "intellectual property crime is taking place on a vast scale globally. Many serious and organized criminals are involved, either

in the manufacture of counterfeit products or in their distribution, attracted by the high profits, the low risk of detection and the fact that penalties are rarely more than minimal" (Alliance Against Counterfeiting and Piracy 2003).

2 For general discussion see Nasheri (2004).

3 Operation Green Quest—a multi agency task force established by the Treasury Department and aimed at identifying, disrupting and dismantling the terrorist financial infrastructure and sources of funding-has specifically recognized counterfeit merchandise schemes as a source of terrorist funding (United States Department of Treasury 2001).

4 Paramilitary groups in Northern Ireland funded their terrorist activities through the sale of pirate products, including the sale of the Lion King (Millar 2002).

5 Recovered Al-Qaida terrorist training manuals revealed that the organization recommends the sale of fake goods as one means to raise funds to support terrorist operations (Von Radowitz 2002).

6 In 1996, the FBI confiscated 100,000 counterfeit t-shirts bearing fake and unauthorized Nike "swoosh" and/or Olympic logos that were intended to be sold at the 1996 summer Olympic games. The operation generated millions of dollars and was run by the followers of sheik Omar Abdel Rahman—a blind cleric who was sentenced to 240 years in prison for plotting to bomb New York City landmarks (Mintz and Farah 2002).

7 In 1996 Business Week reported that the FBI had investigated the link between counterfeit merchandize sales in New York and the terrorists who bombed the World Trade Center in 1993 (Stern 1996).

8 In addition to their other crimes, some terror groups are also quite successful at counterfeiting United States currency.

9 This same article noted that Hezbollah traffics in counterfeit pharmaceuticals.

10 See section 182 of the Omnibus trade and Competitiveness Act of 1988, 19 USC § 2242 ("Special 301"). Pursuant to this statute, the USTR is required to issue an annual report that identifies and categorizes those countries that deny adequate and effective protection and enforcement of intellectual property (IP) rights. See also 2003 Submission of the International Anti-Counterfeiting Coalition, Inc. to the United States

Trade Representative, Special 301 Recommendations (February 13, 2003) available at http://www.iacc.org/teampublish/uploads/Final301-03.pdf (providing background information regarding the scope of the intellectual property problems in this region. Copies of the USRT Special 301 reports from 2000 through 2002 are available at (http://www.ustr.gov/sectors/intellectual.shtml).

11 Counterfeit operations in Paraguay tri-border region may have been used to raise money to support terrorist operations and groups (Feds Track Counterfeit Goods and Sales 2004).

12 Larry Johnson, former Deputy Director of the Office of Counterterrorism for the United States State Department testified on Capital Hill that he was involved in an investigation that uncovered product counterfeiting by radical Palestinian groups in Cuidad del Este, near the tri-border area (Global Options Inc. and Reconnaissance International Report 2003).

13 Paramilitary groups in Northern Ireland funded their terrorist activities through the sale of pirate products, including the sale of the Lion King (Millar 2002).

REFERENCES

Alliance Against Counterfeiting and Piracy. 2003. "Proving the Connection, Links between Intellectual Property Theft and Organized Crime." Retrieved March 22, 2004 (http://www.aacp.org.uk/Proving-the-Connection.pdf).

Federal Bureau of Investigation Homepage, the Financial Institution Fraud Unit, Intellectual Property Crimes. 2204. Retrieved March 25, 2004 (http://www.fbi.gov/hq/cid/fc/fifu/about/about_ipc.htm).

International Anti-Counterfeiting Coalition. 2003. "Get the Facts on Fakes! Violent Crime and the Link to Knock-Offs." Retrieved February 28, 2003 (http://www.iacc.org/tearnpublish/109_476_l676.CFM).

Glaberson, W. 2003. "6 are Charged with Selling Millions of Counterfeit Marlboros." *The New York Times*, February, 21, p. B3.

Global Options, Inc. & Reconnaissance International Report. 2003. "An Analysis of Terrorist Threats to America's Medicine Supply," May 22. Washington, D.C.

Goldberg, J. 2002. "In the Party of God: Hezbollah Sets up Operations in South America and the United States," *The New Yorker*, October 28, vol. 78, p. 74.

Grant, Iain. 2003. Statement to the House Committee of International Relations. *International Federation of the Phonographic Industry, Music Piracy: Organized Crime and Links with Terrorism*, July 16. House Committee of International Relations, Washington, DC.

Hearing of the House International Relations Committee. 2003. *Intellectual Property Crimes: Are Proceeds from Counterfeited Goods Funding Terrorism*, July 16. Retrieved March 25, 2004 (www.fnsg.com).

Hutchinson, Asa. 2003. Statement before the House International Relations Committee. *Intellectual property crimes: are proceeds from counterfeited goods funding terrorism?* July 16. Retrieved March 25, 2004 (www.fnsg.com).

Hyde, Henry J. 2003. Opening Remarks before the hearing on Committee on International Relations. *Intellectual Property Crimes: Are Proceeds from Counterfeited Goods Funding Terrorism?* July 16. Retrieved March 25, 2004 (www. fnsg.com).

Johnson, Larry C. 2003.Testimony before the hearing on Committee on International Relations. *Hearing on intellectual property crimes: Are proceeds from counterfeited goods funding terrorism?* July 16. Retrieved March 25, 2004 (www.fnsg.com).

Junger, S. 2002. "Terrorism's New Geography," *Vanity Fair* 508(December):8.

Kaihla, P. 2002. "Forging Terror, How Rapid Advances in Scanning, Printing, and other Technologies have Made Counterfeiting a Potent New Weapon of Holy War." *Business 2.0*, December 2. Retrieved March 15, 2004 (http://www.business2.com/b2/web/articles/0,17863,515206,00.html).

Lantos, Tom. 2003. "Statement on Intellectual Property Crimes and Terrorism," July 15. *Democratic Office Statement*, Washington, DC.

Llorito, D.L. 2003a. "Loose Rules make CD Pirates Feel at Home Here," January 2. *The Manila Times*, Internet Edition. Available at (http://www.manilatimes.net/others/special/2003/jan/02/20030102spe1.html).

Llorito, D.L. 2003b.). "Lax Rules Give CD Pirates a New Home in the Philippines." *The Straits Times*," January 6. Internet Edition. Available at (http://www.cdfreaks.com/news2.php?ID=5460).

Malcolm, John G. 2003. "Federal Document Clearing House Congressional Testimony," March 13. *The Internet, and Intellectual Property Committee on the House Judiciary, Copyright Piracy and Links to Crime and Terrorism*, Washington, DC.

Marzulli, J. 2003. "Fake Marlboro Men Busted in Smuggling Ring," *Daily News*, February 2, p. 37.

Millar, K. 2002. "Paramilitary Groups in Northern Ireland Funded their Terrorist Activities Through the Sale of Pirate Products, including the Sale of the Lion King," November. *Financing Terror: U.S. Customs Service Monthly Newsletter*. Retrieved March 25, 2004 (http://www.customs.gov/custoday/nov2002/index.htm).

Mintz, J. and D. Farah. 2002. "Small Scams Probed for Terror Ties," *The Washington Post*, August 12, p. A1.

Nasheri, H. 2004. *Economic Espionage and Industrial Spying*. Cambridge University Press: New York and London.

Nurton J. 2002. September. "Why Counterfeiting is Not so Harmless." *Managing Intellectual Property* 122:43.

Trainer, Timothy. 2003. "Prepared Testimony before the Committee on International Relations." *Global Intellectual Property Theft: Links to Terrorism and Terrorist Organizations*, July 16. Retrieved March 25, 2004 (www.fnsg.com).

Roig-Franzia, M. 2002. "N.C Man Convicted of Aiding Hezbollah, Cigarette Smuggling Scam to Fund Terror." *The Washington Post*, June 22, p. A.11.

Rother, L. 2002. "South America Region Under Watch for Signs of Terrorists." *The New York Times*, December 15, p. 32.

Solomon, J. 2002. "Feds Track Counterfeit Goods and Sales," October 24. Retrieved March 25, 2004 (http://www.highbeam.com/library).

Sommerlad, N. 2000. "Two Arrested After Police Find Explosives," December 20. *Press Association.* Available at (http://www.customs.gov/custoday/nov2002/index.htm).

Stern, W. 1996. "Why Counterfeit Goods may Kill." *Business Week,* 3491(September):6.

Taylor, L. 2003. "Big Business Targets Terrorist Pirates." *Australian Financial Review*, January 29, p. 9.

United States Department of State. 2000. "Patterns of Global Terrorism 2000." Retrieved April 30, 2001 (http://www.state.gov/s/ct/rls/pgtrpt/2000/2437.htm).

United States Department of Treasury. 2001. "Green Quest, Finding the Missing Piece of the Terrorist Puzzle." Retrieved March 25, 2004 (http://www.customs.ustreas.gov/xp/cgov/enforcement/investigative_priorities/greenquest.xml).

Valenti, J. 2003. Testimony of Jack Valenti Before the Subcommittee on Courts, the Internet, and Intellectual Property Committee on the Judiciary U.S. House of Representatives "International Copyright Piracy: Links to Organized Crime and Terrorism," March 13. Retrieved (http://www.copyrightassembly.org/briefing/test_2003_03_13.pdf).

Von Radowitz, J. 2002. "Fake Internet Goods 'Linked to Terrorists,'" June 25.

Chapter 4

HUMAN TRAFFICKING IN THE UNITED STATES: UNCOVERING THE NEEDS OF VICTIMS AND THE SERVICE PROVIDERS WHO WORK WITH THEM

Heather J. Clawson, Kevonne Small,
*Ellen S. Go, and Bradley W. Myles**

Although there is a growing amount of literature on the causes and practices of trafficking, little information currently exists on the needs of trafficking victims and the service providers working to meet those needs. Furthermore, the knowledge-base about the needs of service providers and trafficking victims is largely anecdotal and fragmented. While data exists among the organizations that provide services to trafficking victims, few of these organizations analyze the information they collect. In addition, these data lack uniformity across organizations, making it difficult to analyze in a systematic fashion. Since the passage of the Victims of Trafficking and Violence Protection Act of 2000 in the United States, it is important for those involved in the U.S. criminal justice system to better understand the needs of trafficking victims and the barriers and challenges faced by service providers to better respond to cases of human trafficking. To help educate the field on this issue and to address the current

* Caliber Associates 10530 Rosehaven Street, Suite 400, Fairfax, Virginia 22030, www.caliber.com. We would like to acknowledge the support of the National Institute of Justice, U.S. Department of Justice under contract number OJP-99-C-010. Also, we would like to thank all of the service providers and trafficking victims who participated in the study.

lack of systematic data collection regarding the needs of service providers and trafficking victims, Caliber Associates, Inc. conducted a national needs assessment of service providers and trafficking victims in the United States to determine:

- What services currently exist for trafficking victims?
- How responsive are these services to victims?
- What barriers exist to providing/accessing services?
- What support do service providers need to effectively serve trafficking victims?

This chapter begins with a review of current literature on the issue of trafficking in persons in the United States, continues with a description of the methodology and presentation of the key findings from the study, and concludes with suggestions for future research.[1]

Current Literature on Trafficking in Persons in the United States

Human Trafficking Defined

The United States Congress defines trafficking in persons as all acts involved in the transport, harboring, or sale of persons within national or across international borders through coercion, force, kidnapping, deception, or fraud, for purposes of placing persons in situations of forced labor or services, such as forced prostitution, domestic servitude, debt bondage, or other slavery-like practices (Victims of Trafficking and Violence Protection Act of 2000, 22. U.S.C. §7101b). Whether or not an activity falls under this definition of trafficking depends on two factors: the type of work victims are forced to perform and the use of coercion, force, kidnapping, deception, or fraud to secure that forced work.

The crime of trafficking in persons receives its name because the perpetrators often move or "traffic" victims from their home communities to other areas—either domestically within the country of origin or to foreign countries—to profit from their forced labor (Department of State 2002). Victims are often brought to areas where the demand for such forms of labor is highest and most consistent, such as large cities, vacation and tourist areas, or near military bases (Miko 2000). Also, in many cases, the trafficker charges the unknowing victim an exorbitant smuggling fee or "employment" fee. These fees range anywhere from hundreds to thousands of dollars. When the victim cannot pay this fee up front, the trafficker locks the victim in a vicious cycle of debt bondage or indentured servitude that prevents victims from ever paying off the original fee (O'Neill-Richard 1999). This aspect of indentured servitude has led many to characterize human trafficking as modern day slavery. Traffickers capitalize on victims' indebtedness and isolation and combine the use of threats, intimidation, manipulation, and violence to control victims, break their will, confine them in captivity, and force them to engage in sex acts or to labor under slave-like conditions (Department of State 2002). Types of trafficking include forced begging, bonded labor, forced prostitution, servile marriage, false adoption, domestic servitude, and work in sweatshops. In addition, trafficking may also feed into the industries of agriculture, food processing, pornography, sex tourism and entertainment, construction, organ harvesting, and restaurant work.

Explanations for the Existence of Trafficking in Persons

The crime of trafficking in persons affects virtually every country in the world (Miko 2000). This trade in humans occurs on a global scale, but due to its covert and underground nature, the international magnitude of the problem is difficult to ascertain. A recent estimate from United States Government suggests that approximately 800,000 to 900,000 persons are trafficked across international borders each year (Department of State 2003). Traffickers often prey on impoverished individuals who are frequently unemployed or underemployed and who lack access to social safety nets, such as women and children from certain countries and cultures (U.S. Department of Labor 2002). Trafficking victims are deceived into enticing employment agreements through false promises of economic opportunities that await them in more affluent destination countries, such as the United States. Hence, patterns and routes of trafficking often flow from less developed countries to neighboring countries or industrialized nations with higher standards of living. Victims are most commonly lured from third world countries in Asia, Eastern Europe, Africa, and Latin America that display consistently high rates of poverty, violence, and corruption (Modern Day Slavery 2002). Economic and political instability, government corruption, illiteracy, civil unrest, low food production, high infant mortality rates, and internal armed conflict within a country all represent various indicators or "push" factors that increase the likelihood that a country will become a source of trafficking victims (Department of State 2002).

Individual traffickers and the networks of international organized crime are attracted to the trade in humans because of low risk of prosecution and because the criminal penalties for sex trafficking are light in most countries (Tiefenbrun 2002). Traffickers perceive that they operate with ostensible impunity. The *Trafficking in Persons Report-June 2003* reiterates this point about light criminal penalties and describes how traffickers enjoy "virtually no risk of prosecution" by using dramatic improvements in transportation and communications to run their international trafficking operations. The report indicates that traffickers avoid punishment for their crimes by operating in locations where there is little rule of law, lack of enforcement of anti-trafficking laws, and corruption of government and law enforcement institutions (Department of State 2003).

Moreover, trafficking is uniquely lucrative because traffickers can receive steady profits from repetitious forced labor or sexual exploitation for prolonged periods of time, as compared to smugglers who often receive only one payment for transporting one person (O'Neill-Richard 1999). Unlike the sale of drugs, human victims can be sold repeatedly, which creates high profit margins for perpetrators (Cooper 2002).

Furthermore, the practice of trafficking does not require a large capital investment on the part of the trafficker. As a result, the crime of trafficking in persons offers international organized crime syndicates a low-risk opportunity to make billions in tax-free profits by exploiting a system of seemingly unlimited supply and unending demand for a relatively low cost (Mafia 2000). The Vienna-based International Centre for Migration Policy Development estimates that overall profits from trafficking in persons totaled as much as $7 billion in 1995 (Bimal 1998). More recent estimates suggest that overall profits from the crime have increased to approximately $9 billion (Vital Voices 2003).

The Trafficking in Persons Problem in the United States

In the *Trafficking in Persons Report-June 2003*, the United States Department of State suggests that approximately 18,000 to 20,000 people are trafficked into the United States each year for the purposes of forced labor, involuntary domestic servitude, and/or sexual exploitation (excluding internal trafficking within U.S. borders) (Department of State 2003). Moreover, the 2002 edition of this report asserts that the United States is principally a transit and destination country for the practice of human trafficking (Department of State 2002). The Bureau of Immigration and Customs Enforcement (BICE) has identified numerous brothels throughout the United States that likely involved at least several trafficking victims (O'Neill-Richard 1999). Investigative findings such as this one, combined with media stories and government reports, indicate that trafficking for sexual and commercial exploitation is a growing domestic problem that annually increases in scope and magnitude.

While some trafficking victims do enter into the United States through legal means, many trafficking victims are transported across America's borders in a variety of clandestine ways, such as by plane, boat, car, train, or on foot (Raymond and Hughes 2001). Traffickers also deceive BICE personnel by bringing women and children in under the guises of educational visas, tourist visas, false marriage, or fraudulent entry papers (see Siegel in this issue). Furthermore, traffickers operate in the United States because they perceive a low risk of prosecution or deterrence from the American criminal justice system. A review of human trafficking court cases revealed that criminal penalties for traffickers appear light and harmless compared to sentences given to drug or weapons dealers. For example, the statutory maximum for sale into involuntary servitude is only ten years per count as part of the Trafficking Victims Protection Act (TVPA), whereas the statutory maximum for dealing ten grams of LSD or distributing a kilo of heroin is life in prison. Moreover, previously convicted traffickers charged with forced prostitution and forced servitude have received relatively light sentences, ranging from a mere seven months to fifteen years in prison (O'Neill-Richard 1999).

Due to egregious human rights violations and the increased impact on the domestic front, the issue of trafficking in persons has received widespread U.S. attention within the last decade. Unfortunately, conditions are ripe for the trafficking industry to continue to thrive in the United States due to weak economies, unemployment, and scarce job opportunities in foreign countries of origin, the low risk of prosecution and enormous profit potential for traffickers, and improved international transportation and communication infrastructures (Raymond and Hughes 2000).

Responses to Trafficking in Persons: United States Federal Legislation

Because the crime and effects of human trafficking have only recently become salient issues, the United States' response to the issue is still in its nascent stages. However, noticeable progress has been made over a relatively short period of time. For example, Congress passed pioneering national legislation with the Victims of Trafficking and Violence Protection Act of 2000, an act composed of three separate divisions (Candes 2001). Division A of this Act is the Trafficking Victims Protection Act of 2000, commonly referred to as the TVPA. The TVPA is the first comprehensive United States law to address the various complexities of human trafficking practices.[2] Based on a three-tiered framework of prevention, prosecution, and protection, the TVPA was formulated to reduce the imbalance between the severity of the crime and the average length of criminal sentences, to rectify the inadequacy of past United States' laws, and to begin to systematically and explicitly combat the issue of trafficking in persons within the United States. As it is stated in the Act, the purpose of the TVPA is to

> combat trafficking in persons, a contemporary manifestation of slavery whose victims are predominantly women and children, to ensure just and effective punishment of traffickers, and to protect their victims. The TVPA also recognized that, before its enactment, 'existing legislation and law enforcement in the United States and other countries are inadequate to deter trafficking or to bring traffickers to justice, failing to reflect the gravity of the offenses involved.' (TVPA 2000:22 U.S.C. 7101a)

As one prevention strategy in the TVPA, Congress directed the President to establish and implement international initiatives to enhance economic opportunities for potential trafficking victims. Examples of these initiatives include micro-lending programs, job training and counseling, educational programs, public awareness programs, and grants to nongovernmental organizations (NGOs) to accelerate and advance the political, economic, social, and educational roles of women in their home countries. In addition, the TVPA also augments prevention efforts by providing for the allocation of federal grant funds to be set aside for research and evaluation to further explore the practices and effects of the crime (TVPA 2000: 22 U.S.C. 7104-5).

The TVPA, along with the Immigration and Nationality Act, endeavors to provide federal prosecutors with a stricter base of statutes under which to prosecute human trafficking offenses. For example, the TVPA provides the first definition under Federal law of a "victim of trafficking," and it broadens the definition of involuntary servitude as defined by the Supreme Court in *United States v. Kozminski* (Cooper 2002). The Immigration and Nationality Act also creates stiffer penalties for trafficking with respect to peonage, slavery, involuntary servitude, or forced labor. After the passage of the Immigration and Nationality Act, these crimes now carry a maximum prison term of 20 years (18 U.S.C. 1590 2003). Also, if any of these acts results in death, or the crime includes kidnapping and/or aggravated sexual abuse, the defendant can be imprisoned for any term of years to life in prison. Moreover, the maximum prison term for the crime of sex trafficking of children by force, fraud or coercion is now 40 years (18 U.S.C. 1591 2003).

To protect victims, the TVPA creates new standards of eligibility for trafficking victims to receive government benefits under Federal or State programs, regardless of their potentially illegal or undocumented status (Protection Project 2001). To implement the vision outlined in the TVPA, the Federal Departments of Justice (DOJ) and Health and Human Services (HHS) are working together to certify hundreds of trafficking victims through the Office of Refugee Resettlement (ORR), so that to the same extent as refugees, trafficking victims may receive a wide range of Federal and State benefits including employment authorization, housing, mental-health services, medical care, and Supplemental Security Income (SSI).[3] The TVPA also provides for the protection of trafficked individuals while they are in the custody of the Federal government or are assisting in the prosecution of a Federal case.[4] In this regard, the TVPA creates eligibility for victims of trafficking to enter the Federal Witness Security Program, which is outlined in and regulated by the Victim and Witness Protection Act (22 U.S.C. 7105 c1 2000).

The Immigration and Nationality Act also provides protection to human trafficking victims by granting victims a T-visa that gives them temporary residency status in the United States. To be eligible for a T-visa, trafficking victims must meet certain criteria including: (a) that the victim is or has been a victim of a severe form of trafficking in persons as defined in section 7102(8) of the TVPA; (b) the victim is physically present in the

United States, American Samoa, or the Commonwealth of the Northern Mariana Islands, or at a port of entry thereto, on account of such trafficking; (c) the victim has complied with requests for help in the investigation or prosecution of traffickers or has not reached the age of 15; and (d) the victim would suffer extreme hardship involving unusual or severe harm upon removal from the United States. In addition, the Immigration and Nationality Act outlines criteria for the protection of the families of trafficking victims as well. The Immigration and Nationality Act allows the United States Attorney General to grant derivative T-visas to the victim's spouse and children, and to the victim's parents if the victim is less than 21 years of age (Protection Project 2001; 8 U.S.C. 1101 a15T 2000). These provisions signify a shift in United States' policy, which previously subjected illegal aliens to deportation, irrespective of the circumstances that brought them to the country (Protection Project 2001).

The TVPA also created new mandates for numerous Federal agencies that would necessarily be involved in some aspect of response to the crime. The TVPA lays out new guidelines for the Departments of State, Justice, Labor, and Health and Human Services to respond to human trafficking in various preventive, protective, and investigative ways. For example, the TVPA calls for the establishment of an Interagency Task Force to Monitor and Combat Trafficking supported by a new office within the Department of State.[5] In addition, the TVPA requires the Secretary of State, with the assistance of the Interagency Task Force, to submit an Annual Report to Congress on the status of certain aspects of trafficking in persons, such as different countries' efforts to address and combat the issue. Finally, the TVPA recognizes that combating the global issue requires international cooperation between countries of origin, transit, and destination. To this end, the TVPA sets minimum standards for the elimination of trafficking that other countries must satisfy, offers assistance to these countries to meet these standards, and outlines punishments to be taken against countries that fail to meet minimum thresholds, such as economic sanctions (Protection Project 2001). Overall, the passage of the TVPA represents a bold step taken by the United States government to begin to address the crime of trafficking in persons both domestically and internationally.

Although the TVPA is widely regarded as a positive step toward addressing the global crime of trafficking in persons, scholars have offered various critiques and posed numerous questions surrounding certain structural aspects of the Act. With regard to the international standards and minimum thresholds that it sets for other countries, the TVPA has been accused of being culturally imperialistic by imposing United States' requirements and values on other countries and cultures. Academic researchers have noted the lack of an enforcement arm built into the TVPA and question whether the Act will have the power to truly operationalize and enforce its three-pronged strategy of prevention, prosecution, and protection. These critics point out that while the Act has the potential to do much good, there is no guarantee that its provisions will be enforced. Similarly, some voice concern about high burdens of proof being placed on victims and the strict eligibility requirements to obtain a T-visa that are built into the TVPA (Tiefenbrun 2002). Other pieces of international legislation require less strict burdens of proof.

The TVPA has further been criticized for not providing adequate means of financial restitution for victims because it omits the awarding of actual and punitive damages, attorney's fees, and litigation expenses to victims (Hyland 2001). Alternatively, some question whether the TVPA can appropriately balance the human rights of trafficking victims with law enforcement obligations. The crime-fighting mechanism in the TVPA compromises the protection and assistance needs of trafficking victims (Hartsough 2002). Some suggest that the protection and services infrastructure that exists for other victims of crime in the United States, such as domestic violence, has not yet been applied to victims of trafficking (Hyland 2001).

Many critical questions surrounding the impact of the TVPA also remain unanswered in the areas of available services, funding, international standards, and the T- visa. Having been in existence for only a few years, the true impact of the TVPA may be determined once further regulations are produced, implemented, and studied, such as the Reauthorization of the TVPA, entitled the Trafficking Victims Protection Reauthorization Act (TVPRA).

The TVPRA maintains many of the same purposes and standards as the TVPA. However, it does enact certain critical modifications. Under the Trafficking Victims Protection Reauthorization Act (TVPRA) there is a greater shift in responsibility to law enforcement agencies. For example, the Reauthorization allows the Department of Health and Human Services (HHS) to consider statements from local and State law enforcement officials that trafficking victims have been complying with the investigation and prosecution of trafficking cases in considering the certification of a trafficking victim. Prior to the Reauthorization, statements were only accepted from Federal law enforcement officials. Also under the Reauthorization, certain dependents of victims, including spouses and minor children, are eligible to receive benefits and services necessary for safety and protection (e.g., housing or shelter assistance, food assistance, health-care assistance, etc.). Further, the TVPRA appropriates FY 2004 and 2005 grant funding for continued federal research, evaluation, and technical assistance efforts.

Responses to Trafficking in Persons: State and Local Social Service Agencies

State and local social service providers also play a role in the response to the crime of trafficking in persons. For example, trafficking victims may require services from city hospitals and city and State Health Departments for numerous physical and mental health needs. As collaboration among providers increases to meet the multiple needs of trafficking victims, social service agencies offer another important resource and are often included in the overall nexus of necessary services.

As the various sectors of providers have gained more knowledge of the necessary elements of meeting the needs of trafficking victims, a concurrent recognition has occurred that no one agency can do it alone. Not only do trafficking victims present a comprehensive host of needs, but also trafficking investigations and prosecutions require the coordination of efforts from a multitude of Federal, State, and local agencies. These agencies may include law enforcement entities, government agencies, health services, mental-health organizations, legal services, nongovernmental organizations, shelters, and social service providers (Post 2002). In response to the need for collaboration, many major cities have formed city-wide task forces to address the trafficking problem in their particular locale. Examples of cities that have task forces include Atlanta, Chicago, Dallas, Houston, Los Angeles, Miami, New York, Seattle, and San Francisco.

Responses to Trafficking in Persons: Nongovernmental Organizations

Numerous U.S.-based and international nongovernmental organizations (NGOs) have taken up the cause of trafficking in persons and are addressing the issue from multiple angles ranging from direct service to policy research. For example, domestic violence shelters, sexual assault clinics, human rights advocates, and/or refugee services provide various direct services to trafficking victims whom they have encountered in their work with other victim populations. Local advocacy and cultural organizations designed to serve a particular ethnic group also may encounter trafficking victims in their work and community outreach. Because human trafficking is a complex, multi-dimensional, and often an international crime, trafficking victims present characteristics and needs that overlap and can fit into many areas of service including domestic violence, immigration, legal, health, and/or mental-health services. Consequently, because many service agencies specialize in one particular area, these agencies collaborate and piece services together to best meet the numerous needs of trafficking victims (Post 2002).

Other NGOs that do not provide direct services to trafficking victims also play an important role in the response to the crime of trafficking in persons. These organizations may provide policy research, legislative advocacy, information dissemination, or public awareness campaigns. For example, Vital Voices, a global partnership NGO that supports women's issues, has partnered with the United Nations Office on Drugs and Crime to launch a global television campaign to combat human trafficking (Vital Voices 2003). Public service announcements (PSAs) produced by this partnership have aired in over thirty-five countries and are being distributed to broadcasters throughout the United States. Through the combined efforts of NGOs, a coordinated infrastructure of services for trafficking victims is growing in response to the crime.

Responses to Trafficking-in-Persons: Faith-based Organizations

Faith-based organizations have mobilized to help address the trafficking-in-persons problem in the United States in various ways. First, two national faith-based agencies, the United States Conference of Catholic Bishops (USCCB) and the Lutheran Immigration and Refugee Services, administer the Federal government's resettlement program for unaccompanied refugee minors (Ryan 1997). The program was formed in the late 1970s and early 1980s and was originally intended solely for the care of unaccompanied refugee entrant minors. The Department of Health and Human Services Office of Refugee Resettlement (ORR) works with these two national faith-based agencies to expand their services to offer shelter and resettlement services to trafficking victims who are minors.

In addition to administering this national resettlement program, faith-based organizations also offer a variety of general social services to trafficking victims. Both of the aforementioned agencies attempt to meet the needs of trafficking victims through the provision of immigration and refugee services, legal services, and services for basic needs such as food, clothing, and shelter. Because these agencies have multiple locations throughout the country, the USCCB and the Lutheran Immigration and Refugee Services play a valuable and integral role in responding to trafficking in persons.

Needs Assessment Methodology

The needs assessment research design incorporated multiple methods, including a national telephone survey and focus groups with service providers and trafficking victims. In the absence of a formal directory of service providers who work with trafficking victims, a snowball sampling technique was employed and 311 service providers were contacted for the telephone survey. The study yielded 98 completed interviews and 61 nonresponses (7 refusals and 54 noncontacts).[6] Subsequent focus groups were used to explore patterns in the telephone survey data and to gather richer qualitative data about the needs of both trafficking victims and service providers, thereby providing a "check and balance" to the telephone interview data. Two focus groups were held, one with 20 service providers, and another one with 6 victims of human trafficking. Although every effort was made to reach a representative sample of providers working with trafficking victims (e.g., type of agency, type of victim served, geography), the generalizability of the findings has limitations. The results do, however, identify priority issues and pressing needs of both service providers and victims of trafficking.

Needs Assessment Key Findings

The key findings from the *National Needs Assessment of Service Providers and Trafficking Victims* are presented in this section in two parts. In Part One we summarize primary lessons learned about the victim service providers who work with victims of trafficking in persons including: the types of agencies represented in the sample, length of service with trafficking clients, ability to meet trafficking victims' needs, knowledge of trafficking in persons, knowledge of the TVPA, barriers to providing service, and resources needed to do a better job. In Part Two, we summarize what was primarily learned about the victims of human trafficking, which these service providers have worked with in the past, or were working with at the time of the study, including: the victims' countries represented and languages spoken, trafficking victims' needs, and barriers to trafficking victims accessing services.

Part I: Findings about the Victim Service Providers

Type of Agencies Represented in the Sample

The telephone respondents in the national sample represented 22 States and the District of Columbia. As shown in Figure 1, when the sample was aggregated by U.S. region, representation was greatest for the West (33 percent), Northeast (22 percent), and Southeast (20 percent) portions of the country.

While efforts were made to make certain that telephone calls were spread out over the United States, attempts were also made to ensure inclusion of a variety of jurisdictions and types of service organizations that work with this population. Respondents were asked where their programs were based, and answers were then coded into eleven different categories described below and shown in Figure 2.

- Legal—These organizations provide legal services to a wide array of victims and encounter trafficking victims in a legal capacity. This category includes Legal Aid organizations, legal non-profits, District Attorney's offices, and private law firms.
- Health—These organizations provide health services to a wide

Figure 1. Trafficking Needs Assessment Interview Participants

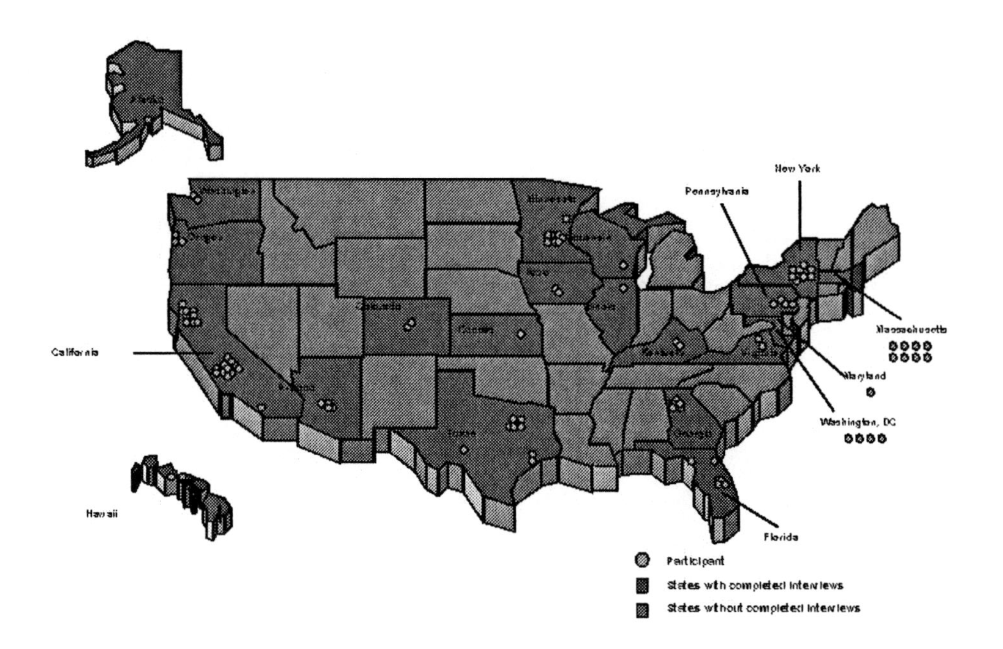

array of victims and encounter trafficking victims in this capacity. This category includes private doctors, clinics, hospitals, and community health centers.

- Education—These institutions provide academic-based services to providers in the form of research assistance, training, and classes or workshops. They also may operate clinics such as legal aid clinics where victims can go for assistance.
- Law enforcement—Law enforcement agencies investigate and report trafficking cases, and provide initial social services through their victims' advocate divisions.
- Immigrant—These organizations serve immigrants, refugees, and asylum-seekers that may require services for a variety of types of victimization, including domestic violence, sexual assault, and torture. They do not necessarily focus their services specifically on trafficking victims, but due to the large overlap between trafficking victims and these other groups, these organizations often serve trafficking victims as well.
- Prostitution recovery services—These organizations serve prostitutes who are either currently prostituting or are trying to recover

Figure 2. Types of Agencies/Organizations Represented in the Sample

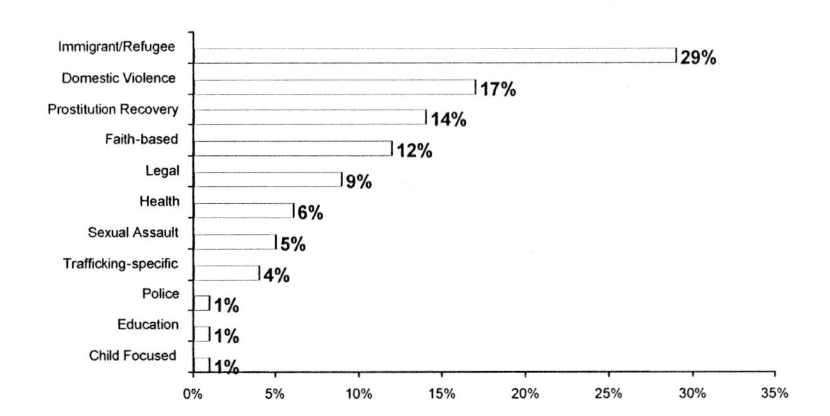

and escape from a life of prostitution. This category encompasses street outreach organizations, prostitution counseling services, and prostitution recovery houses/transitional living houses. These types of organizations encounter victims of sex trafficking.

- Sexual assault—These organizations serve women and children who have been sexually assaulted. Because sexual assault is one potential factor in the overall experience of trafficking victims, these organizations encounter trafficking victims in this capacity.
- Domestic violence—These organizations serve domestic violence victims but occasionally encounter trafficking victims as well. This category includes domestic violence shelters.
- Trafficking—These organizations were created specifically to serve trafficking victims.
- Child-focused services—These organizations focus on serving and providing shelter for children who may be homeless, abused, or victimized in some way. These organizations typically encounter children who have been domestically trafficked or recruited into prostitution.
- Faith-based services—These religiously affiliated organizations may encounter trafficking victims in their service areas, particularly in the areas of immigrant and refugee services, domestic violence, sexual assault, health services, and legal assistance.

Duration of Service

Most respondents reported working with their trafficking victims for more than 12 months. Those providers who worked with trafficking victims for 12 months or more generally served victims who were part of a prosecution; an extremely complicated and lengthy process. Respondents pointed out that, while providers are working with these victims for a year or more, the victim does not necessarily have formal legal status in the United States (i.e., certification) entitling the victim to federal and State benefits. Thus, most respondents who work with victims during their pre-certification period must finance their services and find other providers willing to share some of the financial burden.

Victims who are part of a prosecution tend to stay in one location longer, enabling service providers to work with them for longer periods of time. However, if a trafficking victim is not part of a prosecution, the victim tends to access services intermittently, making it more challenging for providers to move the trafficking victim from a state of vulnerability and dependency to a state of stability and independence.

Ability to Meet Trafficking Victims' Needs

On average, most respondents stated that they were able to meet *some* of the trafficking victims' needs with existing resources and services that they were able to piece together with the help of other service providers. When "ability to meet needs" was broken down by where the service providers' programs are based, it appeared that sexual assault (60 percent) and prostitution recovery services (43 percent) had the greatest difficulty meeting their trafficking victims' needs. Faith-based (17 percent), immigrant (16 percent) and domestic violence (6 percent) organizations also expressed difficulty meeting this population's needs, but less so than other organizations. Respondents working in faith-based, immigrant, and domestic violence organizations suggest that this increased capacity is due to the breadth of comprehensive services provided in-house by these organizations.

Knowledge of Trafficking in Persons

An overwhelming number of respondents (99 percent) reported learning about the issue of human trafficking from their professional work experience. As defined in the study, the category of professional work experience includes direct work with victims (92 percent), interaction with co-workers (65 percent), direct work with other service providers (73 percent), and professional training (36 percent). Respondents reported that these training opportunities were often offered by service providers who have had more experience working with trafficking victims and thus are viewed as relative experts as compared to other service providers who have only recently begun working with trafficking victims.

A reduced amount of providers (35 percent) reported that their trafficking knowledge was obtained from academic sources. For example, respondents cited attending educational trainings, such as clinics on human trafficking or school courses where the topic was explored in class; attending academic conferences; and reading scholarly articles and reports were various means of acquiring academic knowledge. Few respondents (17 percent) gained their knowledge of trafficking from personal experiences (e.g., family member, friend, neighbor, and self). In these few cases, respondents reported talking to other knowledgeable people, talking to survivors, observing the practice for themselves, and having conducted extensive research on the Internet. Overall, 71 percent of respondents reported having attended formal classes or information-based workshops where trafficking was addressed (e.g., domestic violence workshops), while 48 percent reported having received formal skills-based training on how to service trafficking victims.

Respondents were asked to rate the seriousness of trafficking in their area on a five-point scale (1=Not a problem, 3=Somewhat of a problem, 5=Serious problem). Ninety-five percent of respondents described trafficking in their geographic area to be in the range of somewhat of a problem (25 percent) to a very serious problem (45 percent).

Knowledge of the Trafficking Victims Protection Act of 2000

When directly asked about their familiarity with the TVPA, respondents, on average, only felt "somewhat familiar" with the ruling legislation, as shown in Figure 3.

Data suggests that service providers would benefit from training on the existing legislation so that they can more effectively collaborate and communicate with government entities to better serve victims of trafficking.

Figure 3. Familiarity with the TVPA

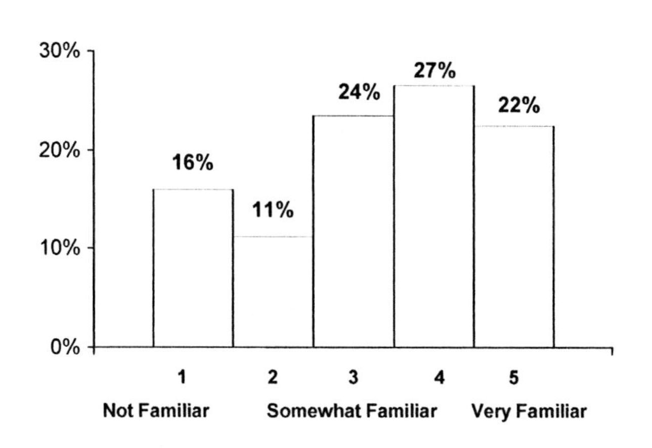

Barriers to Providing Services

Respondents identified key barriers to their ability to provide services to trafficking victims. Figure 4 shows the percentage of service providers who reported having to deal with these common barriers to service.

These barriers are described in more detail below:

- Lack of adequate resources—Need housing/shelter, staff, transportation for victims, contacts in countries of origin, and infrastructures designed for this population;
- Lack of adequate funding—Need source of funding, especially during pre-certification period;
- Lack of adequate training—Need training at all levels on confidentiality issues, how to gain victim trust, outreach methods, how to network and collaborate, cultural/religious competency, identification of victims, how to deal with medical/mental issues, how to service transient populations, and how to manage insufficient number of staff;
- Ineffective coordination with federal agencies—Poor communication and information sharing, poor reporting and prosecution, delays in certification, absence of specialized unit/agency for trafficking, and turf/jurisdictional issues;
- Ineffective coordination with local agencies—Ineffective communication at the State level, ineffective collaboration with local law

Figure. 4 Common Barriers to Providing Services

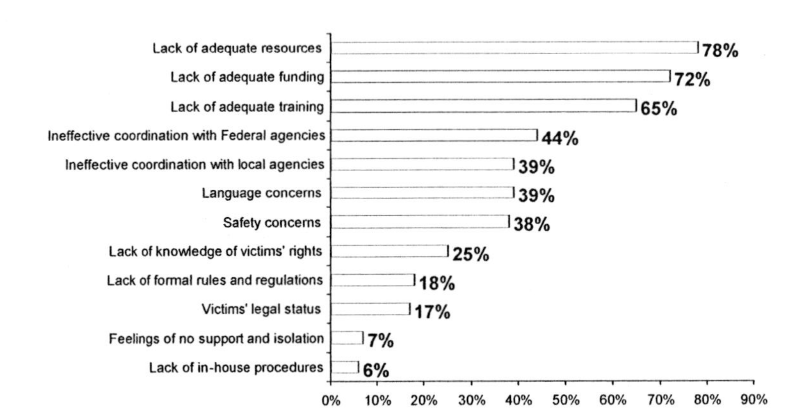

enforcement agencies;

- Language concerns—Not able to readily provide interpreters for all languages/dialects;
- Safety concerns—Safety of victims and staff from trafficking perpetrators;
- Lack of knowledge of trafficking victims' rights—Lack of knowledge/understanding of TVPA, lack of knowledge of trafficking issue in general, lack of awareness among general public;
- Lack of formal rules and regulations—Inadequate or counterintuitive rules, need for legislative advocacy, inadequate victim assistance laws, overly strict eligibility requirements for certification (i.e., requires victims to be certified as "severe forms of trafficking in persons," places the burden of proof on victims, and requires victims' cooperation with law enforcement in order to receive services);
- Victims' legal status—Status renders victim ineligible for social services funding, pre-certification period issues, prior criminal histories;
- Feelings of no support and isolation—Do not know which service providers understand this issue, which providers work with victims of trafficking, and how to collaborate; and
- Lack of in-house procedures—Ineffective protocols, and nonexistent or inadequate data management systems.

Resources Needed to Do a Better Job

Respondents were also asked to identify what they would need to do a better job in providing services to trafficking victims. The needs most often cited include: funding (72 percent), especially for pre-certification services; more training (68 percent) on issues of trafficking, practical information on how to work with trafficking victims and law enforcement, FBI and BICE cultural sensitivity training; collaboration (65 percent) with other service providers and Federal agencies for specific client issues as well as for general support and sharing of lessons learned in service provision; providing and accessing housing or shelter (43 percent); resources (40 percent), such as building space and more staff; community awareness and public education (37 percent); and outreach to victims (31 percent).

Interestingly, categories on this list demonstrate multiple aspects of how service providers view their own needs. Some listed needs are internal to the service providers themselves, such as funding and resources. Other needs relate to ways in which service providers can work together more effectively, such as through cross-training and better collaboration. Greater community awareness and public education about the issue of trafficking represent two external needs that service providers mentioned during the telephone surveys and focus group.

Part II: Findings about the Victims of Trafficking in Persons

Trafficking Victim Population Served

The majority of respondents reported having worked with 20 or more trafficking victims while serving in their current position. The majority (84 percent) of respondents identified clients as trafficking victims by an assessment of the victims' problems. Other methods of identification included the victims' legal status (29 percent), or the victim's self-identification (14 percent). A majority of respondents (89 percent) work with female trafficking victims. Of those working with females, 93 percent reported working with adult women, age 18 and older. Forty-five percent of respondents also reported working with male trafficking victims, who are primarily adults, aged 18 and older. Those respondents who reported working with children (39 percent) work primarily in organizations that focus their efforts on serving children's needs. For some methods of data analysis, the various categories for types of victims served were collapsed into two general categories:

- Sex trafficking victims (80 percent who represent victims of forced prostitution, servile marriage, sex tourism/entertainment, pornography), and
- Labor trafficking victims (68 percent who represent victims forced to act as domestic workers, restaurant/bar workers, sweatshop workers, agricultural workers, bonded laborers, field laborers, food industry, forced begging).

Countries Represented and Languages Spoken

Service providers reported that trafficking victims that they work with come from many different countries. Figure 5 presents the region and percentage of respondents who believe their trafficking victims were from a particular location.

Respondents meet their trafficking clients' language needs in various ways, such as staff, volunteers, interpreter services, victims' family members, other service provider organizations, language banks, or AT&T language lines. Twenty-eight percent of respondents reported meeting all of their trafficking victims' language needs, while 64 percent reported meeting some of their language needs.

Figure 5. Trafficking Victims' Region of Origin

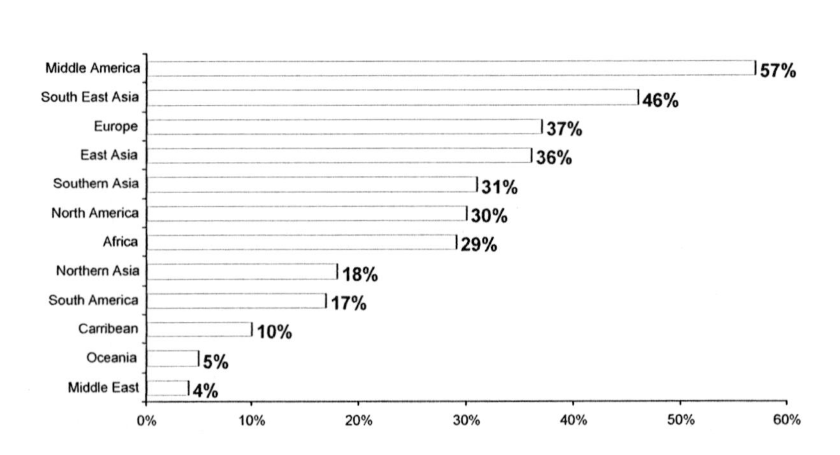

Trafficking Victims' Needs

Respondents reported that trafficking victims were in need of numerous services. Figure 6 illustrates the types of services needed, as reported by service providers.

When the data are separated by type of trafficking victim, it appears that respondents believe labor trafficking victims are most in need of advocacy (97 percent) and medical services (97 percent). The greatest needs of sex trafficking victims seem to be legal/paralegal services (99 percent), medical services (98 percent), and information/referral services (97 percent).

Barriers to Trafficking Victims' Accessing Services

Trafficking victims access services in different ways. A majority of respondents (95 percent) stated that trafficking victims come to their agency/organization through referrals from other service providers or law enforcement. Respondents also noted that victims hear about their services

Figure 6. Trafficking Victims' Needs

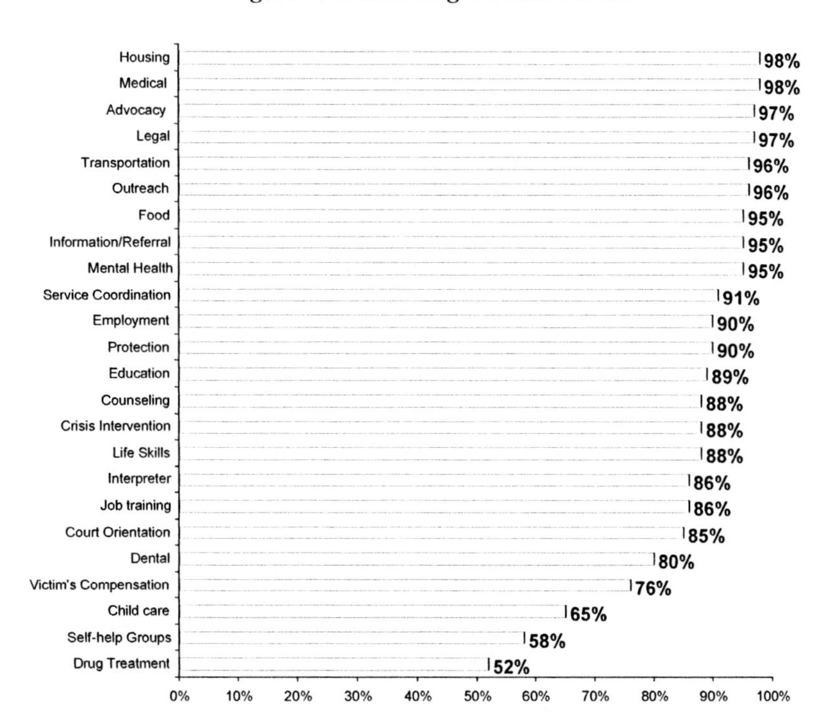

through word of mouth (54 percent) and through community outreach efforts (51 percent). These outreach efforts include street outreach (i.e., presentations around the community) as well as outreach to other agencies/organizations.

Service providers commonly noted the need for improved outreach, as the nature of trafficking is such that victims are not "touching normal mainstreams at all." Respondents also noted the need for improved outreach to service providers, law enforcement, and the general public about trafficking to develop a heightened sense of awareness of the indicators of trafficking. Respondents offered several suggestions for outreach efforts, including public service announcements and media campaigns. To improve outreach to trafficking victims, service providers mentioned making inroads into ethnic communities through the use of ethnic radio, television, and newspapers. In these efforts, respondents noted the importance of being strategic and culturally sensitive in the message that is sent to communities. Finally, respondents observed a need for training among service providers on how to do effective outreach in their areas and locate victims who are "invisible" and "isolated," as well as more resources and staff to devote to outreach efforts. Common reasons cited as to why trafficking victims have difficulties accessing services are shown in Figure 7.

While most of the above categories are self-explanatory, a few of the more nuanced response categories are described here in greater detail. For example, "lack of trust in the system" encompassed victims' reluctance to testify, fear of the law, fear of arrest, fear of government, fear of police, and a belief that government officials have an anti-immigrant sentiment. "Culturally inappropriate services" included responses such as culturally insensitive front-line workers, misunderstood religious beliefs, and cultural differences. The "general fear" category consisted of responses such as brainwashed, learned helplessness, feelings of indebtedness or dependency on perpetrator, mental health issues, fear of the unknown, and lack of self-esteem.

When the data were separated by "type of trafficking victim served," it appears that respondents believe labor trafficking victims are most likely to not access services because they fear deportation (91 percent), and they fear retaliation against themselves or their family members in their home countries (91 percent). According to respondents, sex trafficking victims do not access services primarily because they fear retaliation against themselves and their families (90 percent), and because they are not knowledgeable about available services (85 percent).

Figure 7. Common Barriers to Accessing Services

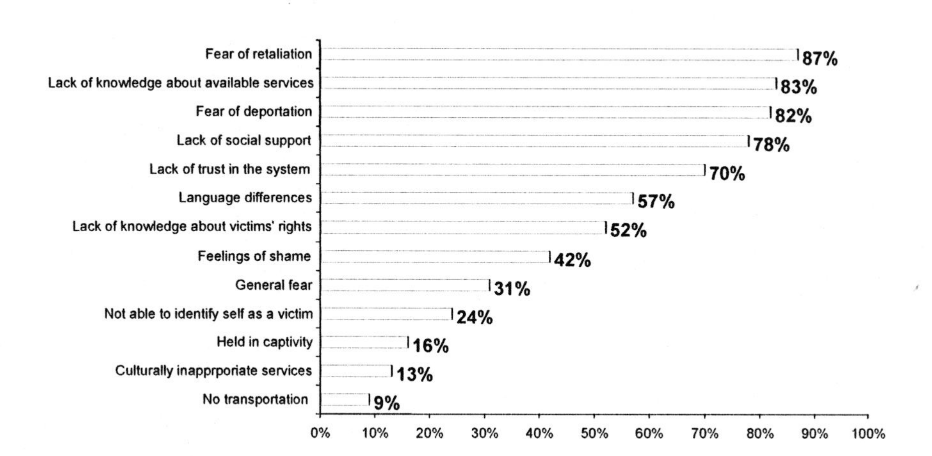

Suggestions for Future Research

This study addresses a significant gap in human trafficking research and provides modest responses to previously unanswered questions. In doing so, the study identifies additional topics that remain unexplored and highlights other pertinent areas for further research. Because a comprehensive and coordinated multi-disciplinary response to the crime of human trafficking is still in its nascent stages, specific future studies that build from this national needs assessment come at a critical juncture. Potential areas for future research are described below.

Sharing of Information between United States and International Service Providers

The numerous agencies that are responding to human trafficking vary in scope and breadth. Some local agencies primarily serve the needs of trafficking victims in a targeted region. Other international agencies/organizations work on a multinational scale to address the root causes of trafficking. An information gap has the potential to emerge between service providers with such varying goals and purposes. However, findings from the needs assessment underscore the untapped strength that resides among these entities—information sharing. Moreover, for agencies that are doing similar work on different scales and in different countries, the sharing of promising practices could foster more effective service provision, both domestically and internationally. Thus, a study that examines the sharing of information between U.S.-based entities and international counterparts could shed light on promising practices for how agencies can work together to best stem the prevalence of trafficking in persons.

Law Enforcement Role in Human Trafficking Cases

The TVPA and the reauthorization of the Act place law enforcement entities in a very important and unavoidable role in the service response to a trafficking case. For example, law enforcement agencies are inextricably interwoven into all three eligibility requirements for an ORR certification letter. Hence, trafficking victims must depend on law enforcement for an endorsement that confirms their cooperation with the criminal investigation and that correctly identifies them as a victim of a "severe form of trafficking in persons." Victims must receive this approval from law enforcement before they can receive a wide array of government-sponsored services such as federal and state benefits. A study that focuses on the impact of the TVPA on law enforcement practices and the role of law enforcement in cases of human trafficking can possess various and important implications for practice. Better victim identification, improved cultural sensitivity and interaction with victims, increased effective prosecution of traffickers, enhanced access to services, and streamlined collaborations between agencies are all potential benefits of a study that focuses on the law enforcement response to human trafficking. Also, it would inform the field on promising practices of how law enforcement should work with other entities involved human trafficking cases.

Assessment of Providers and Victims' Needs in all 50 States and Abroad

As the United States attempts to respond to the growing problem of human trafficking, an important human-rights facet of this response is the provision of services to trafficking victims. A thorough understanding of the services currently available throughout the United States, as well as the services available abroad for those trafficking victims that are repatriated will prove useful. Efforts should be made to conduct a similar needs assessment study that includes more geographical diversity as the provision of services for trafficking victims expands. Continuous learning about the needs of trafficking victims and service providers to best serve this population will only prove to enhance service provision.

Education and Public Awareness of Trafficking in Persons

Despite the documented occurrence of the practice of trafficking in persons in the United States, the results of the needs assessment indicate that service providers perceive a substantial and persistent information gap in public awareness about human trafficking. A study that addresses community education and public awareness efforts both within the United States and abroad could potentially lead to better victim identification, increased vigilance for cases of human trafficking, heightened community sensitivity to the issue, more effective collaboration between service providers, and increased access to services by victims of human trafficking. Public awareness and outreach efforts may include, but are not limited to, brochures, flyers, public service announcements, television commercials, magazine and newspaper articles, community forums, and conferences.

In conclusion, it is clear that human trafficking is a growing international concern and salient issue for both government and nongovernmental organizations. While there are varying opinions regarding the magnitude, causes, and inner-workings of human trafficking, there is widespread agreement that trafficking exists on a global scale, that it will only increase with time, and that urgent responses are necessary to prevent these severe and brutal violations of human rights. As such, there is a critical and timely need for further research in this area to enhance the current understanding of trafficking and to ensure that efforts to combat trafficking are grounded in sound research. Further research will not only inform effective responses for practitioners but will also contribute to policy and legislative development in the areas of human rights, health, gender, law enforcement, and social services. Policies and practices that will, in the final analysis, prevent trafficking, protect trafficking victims, and effectively and appropriately punish trafficking perpetrators.

NOTES

1 This chapter is based on a longer, unpublished study prepared for the National Institute of Justice by H. Clawson, K. Small, E. Go,

and B. Myles (2003), *Needs Assessment for Service Providers and Trafficking Victims*. A copy of the longer study can be obtained from www.caliber.com.

2 See Cooper (2002).

3 *See* generally, 22 U.S.C. §7105(b)(1). Note: Certification is the process by which trafficking victims are granted eligibility to remain in the country for a period of time and receive Federal and State benefits.

4 22.U.S.C. §7105(c)(1).

5 *See* generally, 22 U.S.C. §7103.

6 Refusals are those service providers who declined to participate in the telephone survey. Noncontacts are those service providers whom we attempted to contact at least 5 times but were unable to schedule an interview.

REFERENCES

Candes, M.R. 2001. "The Victims of Trafficking and Violence Protection Act of 2000: Will it become the 13th Amendment of the 21st Century?" *University of Miami Inter-American Law Review* 571:571-603.

Cooper, B. 2002. "A New Approach to Protection and Law Enforcement Under the Victims of Trafficking and Violence Protection Act." *Emory Law Journal* 51:1041-1058.

Department of State. 2002. "Trafficking in Persons Report," June 2002. Available at (www.state.gov/g/tip/rls/tiprpt/2002).

Department of State. 2003. "Trafficking in Persons Report," June 2003. Available at (www.state.gov/g/tip/rls/tiprpt/2003).

Ghosh, Bimal. 1998. *Huddled Masses and Uncertain Shores: Insights into Irregular Migration*. International Organization for Migration (IOM). Available at (www.iom.net).

Hartsough, Tala. 2002. "Asylum for Trafficked Women: Escape Strategies Beyond the T Visa." *Hastings Women's Law Journal* 13(Winter):77.

Hyland, Kelly E. 2001. "Protecting Human Victims of Trafficking: An American Framework." *Berkeley Women's Law Journal* 16:29.

"Mafia Makes Billions from Trafficking People-UN." 2000. *Reuters*, December 15.

Miko, F.T. 2000. "Trafficking in Women and Children: The U.S. and International Response." *Congressional Research Service Report* 98-649 C.

O'Neill-Richard, A. 1999. *International Trafficking in Women to the United States: A Contemporary Manifestation of Slavery and Organized Crime*. Center for the Study of Intelligence. Available at (www.odci.gov/csi/monograph/women/trafficking.pdf).

Post, D. 2002. *What Sexual Assault and Domestic Violence Service Providers Need to Know About Sex Trafficking.* Arizona Department of Health Services Contract No. 961025. AZ: USA.

Protection Project 2001. "Explanation of the Trafficking Victims Protection Act of 2000," The Protection Project Program of Services for Victims of Trafficking. Available at (www.protectionproject.org/training/commentary1.htm).

Raymond, J. and Hughes, D. 2001. Sex Trafficking of Women in the United States. Coalition against Trafficking in Women (www.uri.edu/artsci/wms/hughes/sex_traff_us.pdf).

Ryan, A.S. 1997. "Lessons Learned from Programs for Unaccompanied Refugee Minors." *Journal of Multicultural Social Work* 5:195-205.

Tiefenbrun, S. 2002. "The Saga of Susannah: A U.S. Remedy for Sex Trafficking in Women: The Victims of Trafficking and Violence Protection Act of 2000." *Utah Law Review* 107:107-175.

U.S. Department of Labor. 2002. "Women's Bureau. Trafficking in Persons: A Guide for Non-Governmental Organizations." Available at (www.dol.gov/wb/media/reports/trafficking).

Victims of Trafficking and Violence Protection Act of 2000, 22. U.S.C. §7101(a). Available at (www.ojp.usdoj.gov/vawo/regulations.htm).

Vital Voices 2002. "Modern Day Slavery: Important Information About Trafficking in Persons." Vital Voices Anti-Trafficking Tool-Kit, 2002. Available at (www.vitalvoices.org/programs/antitrafficking/toolkit).

Vital Voices. 2003. "Vital Voices Anti-Trafficking Awareness Campaign." Available at (www.vitalvoices.org/programs/anti-trafficking/anti-trafficking/psa_campaign).

Chapter 5

CASES OF HUMAN TRAFFICKING IN THE UNITED STATES: A CONTENT ANALYSIS OF A CALENDAR YEAR IN 18 CITIES

*Jay Albanese, Jennifer Schrock Donnelly, and Talene Kelegian**

Trafficking in human beings has become one of the most significant crimes of the early twenty-first century, similar to the way that drug trafficking dominated concern about transnational crime during the 1980s and 1990s. Human trafficking continues to draw the attention of many nations. It has been the theme of numerous international conferences, featured in various media, and subjected to national legislation and a binding United Nations protocol connected to the Convention on Transnational Organized Crime.

On the domestic front, human trafficking has become one of the U.S. government's top priorities (Ashcroft 2004). A directive issued on March 11, 1998 by President Clinton launched the beginnings of the U.S. anti-trafficking strategy that was founded on the principles of prevention, protection, support for victims, and the prosecution of traffickers. Since then, the U.S. government response has evolved into a burgeoning anti-trafficking campaign involving multiple federal agencies, local law enforcement, victims groups, immigrants groups, and others. The most notable of these anti-trafficking efforts include: the enactment of anti-traf-

* National Institute of Justice, Washington, D.C., USA (jay.albanese@usdoj.gov) or (jennifer.schrock.donnelly@usdoj.gov).

Opinions or points of view expressed are those of the authors and do not necessarily reflect the position or policies of the U.S. Department of Justice.

ficking legislation; an annual Trafficking in Persons Report (TIP) issued by the U.S. Department of State; increased emphasis and attention to the investigation and prosecution of traffickers; and provision of services for victims and efforts to identify victims.

Defining the Problem

Trafficking in persons can be defined as the recruitment, transportation, transfer, harboring or receipt of persons, by use of force, threat, fraud, or coercion, for the purpose of exploitation, most often involving sexual exploitation or forced labor (United Nations 2004). Current global forces ensure that human trafficking will continue to affect both developed and developing nations. World conditions most commonly cited as contributing factors to international trafficking include developing countries struggling to establish viable economies, a growing number of conflict and post-conflict situations, governments and economies in transition, a globalized economy involving the flow of both legal and illegal products, and the global diffusion of Internet access—which allows an exploitation of supply and demand more quickly than ever.

Since the passage of the first Trafficking Victims Protection Act (TVPA) in 2000, anti-trafficking efforts in the U.S. have resulted in some tangible achievements. By 2003, 111 traffickers had been charged by the U.S. Justice Department (U.S. Department of Justice 2003). However, various international organizations have estimated that hundreds of thousands of people are trafficked every year around the world (see International Organization for Migration 2003). Further, the U.S. government estimates that thousands are trafficked yearly into the United States. The discrepancy between the numbers of estimated victims and the criminal justice response poses a daunting challenge. Clearly, we are lacking extensive information with respect to the scope and nature of the trafficking problem. The need for real information has become critical for the United States and global community to effectively combat this problem: what resources are needed to combat the problem? Where does the problem of human trafficking rank on the list of important social problems? What types of interventions are needed most? Until we can get a better grasp on the numbers and types of victims and traffickers involved, prevention efforts and justice responses will be based more on speculation than fact, and are likely to miss the mark.

The debate regarding the similarities and differences between smuggling and trafficking continues as well. The line between these two transnational crimes is blurred, with much overlap (Denmore 2003). Human trafficking shares certain dynamics with migrant/human smuggling, but it is distinguished by the additional elements of coercion and/or exploitation (Thompson and Ochoa 2004). Migrant smuggling produces short-term profits. Trafficking, on the other hand, can involve a longer period of exploitation to sustain profitability. Generally speaking, the criminality associated with trafficking usually continues after the migrants reach their destinations.

Given the desire of so many to migrate on a global scale, it sometimes becomes difficult to distinguish incidents of human smuggling with human trafficking. This is the case in countries like Algeria, Tunisia, and Egypt, where a large number of illegal migrants transit into Europe. In Algeria for example, transiting illegal immigrants from West and Central Africa travel through the country on their way to European destinations (U.S. Department of State 2003). Consequently, the differing and similar dynamics between human smuggling and trafficking further complicate this already clandestine trade, rendering prevention and interdiction efforts even more difficult. Regardless of the differences, however, it is clear that there are many victims who are caught up in criminal networks attempting to profit from their desire to seek a better life.

The Rise of Human Trafficking as a Transnational Crime Problem

The rapid growth of human trafficking can be accounted for by a combination of five interrelated factors. First, there is a global imbalance in the labor force—with opportunities for employment far fewer than the number of available workers in many developing and post-conflict nations. Second, the role of women in many societies continues to lag, resulting in large numbers of women seeking work (often out of necessity) without a corresponding growth in legitimate opportunities. Third, global communications, especially the Internet, television, and mobile phone access, has made it easier than ever before for those seeking employment and a better life to pursue possibilities outside their own borders. Fourth, many borders opened up after the collapse of the Soviet Union, facilitating easier international travel around the world through conflict and political change. Fifth, transnational organized crime evolved in the early 1990s as a way to smuggle money and property across newly opened borders, thus paving the way for the addition of human beings to this existing flow of trafficked goods and services.

Determining its Scope

The most fundamental step in understanding any problem, following its definition, is an understanding of its nature and scope. How much of this activity occurs? What are its common characteristics?

Ironically, there has been virtually no attention to determining the true extent of trafficking in human beings, despite the general consensus about the seriousness of the problem. The pressing global need to address human trafficking has clearly not been equally matched by research and sufficient information. Specifically, there is little reliable base-line data on the actual volume of trafficking, the operation of criminal networks involved, the illicit market structure, or the effectiveness of various interdiction and prevention strategies. While there are plenty of anecdotal stories from victims and case examples, the true nature and scope of the problem is essentially unknown. How are governments, the public, and the media supposed to understand the problem without knowing the fundamentals behind this crime? How are we to distinguish anecdotal accounts from its true nature? How are we to determine an appropriate level of resources to devote to the problem of human trafficking, in the face of other competing social problems?

There has been much speculation regarding the extent of human trafficking, although no systematic counts have occurred. Current U.S. Government estimates place the number of persons trafficked around the world at 600,000 to 800,000. Beginning in 2001, the U.S. State Department has released an annual report on Trafficking in Persons (TIPS), a report mandated by Congress on the anti-trafficking efforts of governments worldwide. In this report, a 1999 CIA estimate was cited indicating that 45,000 to 50,000 women and children were trafficked into the United States each year. In its 2003 TIPS report, however, the estimate was reduced significantly to 18,000 to 20,000. This estimate, however, was modified once again by the State Department in its 2004 report, with the new estimate indicating 14,500 to 17,500 trafficked annually (U.S. State Department 2004).

Thus, the mystery continues. The basis for the original speculation was never made clear, nor were the reasons for its subsequent downward revisions of more than 50 percent. Thus, we do not know if this reduction was the result of successful prevention/interdiction efforts, better tracking methods, or methodological modifications. Obviously, it is unlikely that a problem of this kind would reduce by more than half in a single year without some kind of dramatic global intervention, which never occurred. If these revisions were in fact the result of a change in methodology, it forces one to question the reliability of the methodology employed, given the significant discrepancies in the original and subsequent revisions since 1999.

It may be more useful and accurate to view these figures as "speculation" rather than "estimates," because estimates are conventionally based on some kind of count. These speculative figures certainly have not been informed by studies that have tried to count actual cases. For example, one study conducted for the National Institute of Justice uncovered 38 documented incidents of trafficking into the United States involving 5,500 women between 1990 and 2000 (Raymond and Hughes 2001). Other actual counts are similarly low, and it is difficult to reconcile actual counts with U.S. government figures (Makkai 2003). This discrepancy is what prompted this analysis, an attempt at a real count, based on actual trafficking incidents in the United States. The result was a content analysis of trafficking arrests as reported in major newspapers over the course of one year in the United States.

Method

The point of departure for the analysis of trafficking cases began with a list of the twenty-five largest cities (by population) in the country, on the assumption that large metropolitan areas are more likely to attract traffickers, smugglers, and illegal migrants. In an effort to obtain a more targeted sample, cities not near a coast or border were deleted, and five cities not on the original list were added (Tucson, Laredo, Buffalo, Miami, and St. Petersburg) because they have, or are near, heavily trafficked ports or borders—presuming that traffickers and their victims are entering the United States most often through metropolitan areas with ports-of-entry. The final list of cities (the additional five cities are in the third column) is as follows:

New York, NY	Boston, MA	Tucson, AZ
Los Angeles, CA	Seattle, WA	Laredo, TX
Chicago, IL	Baltimore, MD	Buffalo, NY
San Diego, CA	Jacksonville, FL	Miami, FL
Detroit, MI	Washington, DC	St. Petersburg, FL
San Francisco, CA	Philadelphia, PA	
San Antonio, TX		

After finalizing the list of cities, a major newspaper in each city was identified.[1] We operated on the assumption that arrests, especially those that involve "hot button" issues such as sex, prostitution, and illegal immigration are usually reported in major newspapers. Therefore, newspaper archives serve as a relatively good record of certain kinds of arrests. It is important to note that cases not resulting in news reports are not included in this analysis.

The methodology for the count began with a search of all dates during calendar year 2002 (January 1, 2002-December 31, 2002) using seven different keywords—given that "human trafficking" is a relatively new term and that many relevant arrests might be excluded from the analysis. The keywords included: "human trafficking," "drug trafficking," "smuggling," "prostitution," "illegal immigration," "alien," and "refugee." Each keyword was searched separately in each cities newspaper over the year. The resulting content analysis included a total of 51 articles in which the arrest appeared to be related to smuggling or trafficking cases.

The content of the smuggling/trafficking articles included methods/modes used to carry out the trafficking, the types of victims, and how entry into the United States was gained. The following definitions were used to identify whether an arrest incident article was smuggling or trafficking (or in some cases, both). For the purposes of the analysis, smuggling was generally defined as the illegal transport of a person into a country. Trafficking was defined using the United Nations definition.[2] As noted earlier, there is a "grey area" between smuggling and trafficking. Articles that mentioned only smuggling were included in the analysis in order to prevent any inadvertent omission of trafficking incidents. Eighteen different variables were used to group and analyze the reports of these arrests:

- Region of United States
- Incident reported (arrest, search, etc.)
- Crime charged
- Underlying crime
- Type of trafficking (prostitution, forced labor, etc.)
- Country of origin
- Entry route (if not directly from original country)
- Number of victims
- Gender of victims
- Age of victims
- Method of entrance into USA
- Type of group facilitating entry
- Victims working to pay off a debt?
- Evidence of trafficking vs. smuggling?
- Lure used to get victim into the USA
- Current status of victim Amount of money paid by the victim
- How police found out about the trafficking/smuggling.

These variables were chosen to elucidate on how traffickers work (i.e., their modus operandi, their methods of recruitment, and how authorities respond). Admittedly, each article did not mention all these variables. However, enough of these factors were addressed to provide a useful data set for analysis.

The data set has several important limitations. Obviously, we can only study what we know exists, so we can only analyze known cases that are officially reported. There are clearly many built-in limitations when using a content analysis approach. We are painfully aware of the likely sizable "hidden" population of trafficked victims that render making estimations inherently problematic. The lack of "official" accounts will no doubt continue to be endemic to human trafficking, simply because things that are difficult to count are often avoided—leading to a dissatisfying array of ever-changing estimates. The data reported here do not reflect cases of trafficking and smuggling that came to the attention of police which did not result in a newspaper report. Although every article had basic information (i.e., who, what, where, and when), some of the articles were not well-researched and were short on facts. This is why the largest category of data is often "information not given." However, even with these significant caveats, there appeared to be enough information in the articles to see patterns emerge from the data at hand and, if not an accurate count of all existing cases, we can get an accurate picture of what many of them are like.

Results

A total of 29 of the 51 (56.8 percent) reports on arrests mentioned the method of entry into the United States. As Table 1 indicates, the most common way to enter the United States was by driving. Traffickers coming from Mexico can drive into the southwestern United States and remain there, or continue on towards the West Coast. Traffickers also drive into the Midwest from Canada. Arriving by boat is also the only documented way that traffickers have used to enter Florida in this sampling of cases.

Table 1 illustrates that air travel is uncommon in these trafficking and smuggling cases, perhaps because of the higher level of post-September 11th security and documentation required, or because this is the costliest option. Victims entering on foot from Mexico are often children, and to avoid detection, some smugglers employ a combination of driving and also taking victims by foot. There are no documented cases of victims walking into the United States from any region other than the Southwest.

Details as to how authorities discovered a specific trafficking and smuggling case were found in only 12 of the 51 cases (23.5 percent). There were three reported methods by which law enforcement learned of a trafficking and smuggling incident: a tip (4 cases), a traffic accident (5 cases), or through a checkpoint (3 cases). Trucks coming from Mexico drive sometimes without headlights, or on back roads, in order to avoid detection—resulting in many accidents, and victims often flee the scene and are not apprehended.

The routes used to gain entry into the United States usually corresponded with geographical convenience related to the source country of the victim, but there are exceptions. Victims from Mexico, Central America, and South America entered through the closest border, the Southwest United States (See Table 2). Most victims from Asia entered through the West Coast. However, sometimes traffickers used more complicated routes

Table 1. Region of United States by Method of Entry into the Country

Region	Entry by Air	On foot	Land (drive)	Water (boat)	Water & Land
Northeast: NYC, Philadelphia, Baltimore, D.C., Boston	1	-	-	1	-
Northwest: Chicago, Detroit, Buffalo	-	-	1	1	1
South: St.Petersburg, Miami	-	-	-	5	-
Southwest: San Antonio, Laredo, Tucson	1	1	9	-	-
West: L.A., San Diego, San Francisco, Seattle	1	1	4	2	-
Totals = 29 (%)	3 (10.3)	2 (6.8)	14 (48.2)	9 (31)	1 (3.4)

to get their victims into the United States, probably in order to avoid detection. Many victims from Russia, Asia, and Africa are routed through Mexico and into the Southwest. In addition, some victims from Mexico and South America are trafficked by air into Canada and then into the United States via the East Coast. Since some documented cases of trafficking neglect to mention the method of entry, and there are also incidents of inter-state trafficking, it is possible that the victims on the East Coast from Mexico ended there after months of being inside the United States.

Few of the traffickers were actually charged with trafficking, probably due to the fact that the TVPA legislation was still in its infancy in 2002. Some were charged with smuggling, conspiracy, racketeering, or a combination of these charges. Most charges in these cases were for smuggling (61 percent), or a combination of smuggling and some other crime. Cases involving multiple charges indicate that traffickers and smugglers can be simultaneously involved in many other illegal activities.

As illustrated in Table 3, most commonly between 11 and 50 victims were involved in trafficking incidents in this sample. This number might be due to the economics and practicalities of the enterprise of human trafficking: groups must be small enough to maintain control, yet large enough to make a profit and justify the risks of smuggling.

Trafficking victims include both genders; 49 percent of the cases in our sample included *both* female and male victims. Trafficking cases

Table 2. Source Country of Victim

U.S. Region	Asia/ Russia	Mexico/ Central America	South America	Europe	Africa
New York, Philadelphia, Baltimore, Washington, D.C., Boston	2	3	1	-	1
Chicago, Detroit, Buffalo	2	1	-	-	-
St. Petersburg, Miami	-	6	-	-	-
San Antonio, Laredo, Tucson	-	16	1	-	-
Los Angeles, San Diego, San Francisco, Seattle	8	8	-	2	-
Totals = 51 (%)	12 (23.5)	34 (66.6)	2 (3.9)	2 (3.5)	1 (1.9)

involving a single sex usually involved females (46 percent) versus males (3 percent). The sample of articles indicated that female victims were usually exploited for purposes of prostitution, whereas males were used primarily for sweatshop labor.

Smugglers brought (all at once) many people of different ages to the United States. Traffickers, however, appeared to be more selective, bringing in either teenagers, children, or adults, and not all ages at the same time. This may be due to the reality of trafficking—given the continued exploitation that occurs after trafficked victims are in the United States, traffickers may have specific jobs in mind for the victims and thus pick their ages accordingly.

Although the details regarding the criminal groups involved in trafficking cases were identified in only 25 cases, the data provide an indication of the nature and types of groups that engage in, support, or facilitate trafficking in human beings. Five different types of groups were identified: corrupt government officials (6), established crime groups (8), family members (6), foreign nationals (3), and non-established crime groups (2). Eighty percent of the cases involved three types of groups: established crime groups (identified as previously active in other crimes), corrupt government officials (border officers, etc.), and family members. This diversity of groups corresponds with studies of trafficking of women from Ukraine which found the process "highly flexible," where criminals adapting quickly "to different opportunities and in response to risks, so traf-

Table 3. Number of Trafficking Victims per Incident

Underlying activity	Unknown Number of victims	1-5 victims	6-10	11-50	51-100	101+
Smuggling	10	5	2	8	2	2
Trafficking	5	1	5	6	-	1
No information given	-	1	-	2	-	1
Totals N=51 (%)	15 (30)	7 (14)	7 (14)	16 (32)	2 (4)	4 (8)

fickers may operate in one way in one region, but differently in another region" (Hughes and Denisova 2004:71; see also Zhao 2003).

Few reports addressed how the victim was lured into the United States. Most victims were promised to be "reunited with family," followed by promises of jobs or money, and promise of marriage or education opportunities. Several existing studies that involve interviews with trafficking victims have shed light on the economic and individual factors that form trafficker-victim agreements, which many times turn out to be false promises (Sellier 2003; Lesko and Avdulaj 2003).

Discussion

Our content analysis was based on a small sample, however, it provides a concrete look at actual cases, types of individuals, and countries involved in trafficking incidents over the course of one year in the United States. The unknowns about human trafficking have forced many assumptions to be made in terms of locating and responding to victims, and the legislative and criminal justice actions taken. With respect to trafficking in persons, policymakers need the knowledge to make well-informed decisions about committing resources and focusing programs where the problems are greatest, and where these resources are likely to do the most good. Obviously, we must continue to invest resources to better understand its true nature and extent (International Organization for Migration 2003). The horrible human consequences that trafficking entails demands it. However, without any baseline information, it is difficult to determine where and how to intervene and launch any substantive proactive efforts to thwart the problem.

Developing a Better Estimate

Are these data misleading? It is hard to say, except that a look at the reporting of the first 3 months of 2003 in the 25 major newspapers from these major cities revealed no increase in the number of cases reported, using the same broad key word search used for the 2002 cases. There are efforts underway to improve training, detection, and investigation on the part of police so that they are better able to distinguish indicators of trafficking activity from traditional prostitution, immigration, and smuggling cases. More experience with new trafficking laws is necessary to determine their efficacy in practice (Tiefenbrun 2002). It will also be important to raise awareness on the part of citizens to be observant for signs of suspicious activity, and understand the seriousness of trafficking in human beings. If successful, these training and awareness-raising activities will result in better knowledge about the true extent of human trafficking.

Furthermore, given the inherently global dimension of human trafficking, local, national and international criminal justice communities must unite in their efforts to achieve better estimates. Naturally, valid and reliable estimates of the human trade can only occur with cross-collaborative and international research efforts behind them. This is paramount to the development of true measures of the success (or not) of anti-trafficking efforts in the United States and across the globe. The international, regional, and national cooperation required to develop trafficking estimates (from source countries through transit countries to destination countries) has begun. Work by the International Office for Migration and United Nations Children's Fund, for example, is collecting first-hand information from the victims through their anti-trafficking activities around the world (International Office for Migration 2003; UNICEF 2004). The United Nations Office of Drugs and Crime is developing a database of known trafficking cases, and the regional Stability Pact Task Force on Trafficking in Human Beings (of the Organization for Stability and Co-operation in Europe) is working to coordinate anti-trafficking efforts and information in southeastern Europe (United Nations 2004a; Stability Pact 2004). These are the kinds of cooperative, information-sharing activities that can be organized and coordinated to develop better national, regional, and global estimates of human trafficking. Although we can and should continue to increase investigations, prosecutions, and liberate victims on an international scale; without more reliable estimates, we cannot know if we are achieving significant reductions or making any real progress. The true extent and nature of international trafficking can only be measured and assessed with data that is cross-national in scope.

Conclusion

The discrepancies among trafficking estimates and ongoing debate about the nature and extent of human trafficking in the United States and around the world will no doubt continue. Admittedly, this content analysis is a modest exploration into the scope of trafficking into the United States. It is, however, an actual count, and provides a window into real cases in the United States. Our goal in this analysis was to contribute to the ongoing dialogue about the nature and impact of trafficking in the United States. As noted above, existing international, regional, and national efforts around the world can be coordinated to derive better estimates, assess trends, and better inform potential victims and policymakers of the true extent of the nature and harm of human trafficking. It is paramount that research continues to advocate for more hard data to inform the appropriate targeting, responses, and resources in the amorphous world of trading in human beings.

NOTES

1 San Antonio Express-News, Laredo Morning Times, Buffalo News, Los Angeles Times, The New York Times, The Miami Herald, Chicago Tribune, Houston Chronicle, Philadelphia Inquirer, The Arizona Republic, San Diego Union Tribune, Detroit Free Press, The Baltimore Sun, San Francisco Chronicle, Florida Times-Union, The Boston Globe, The Seattle Times, Florida Times-Union, Arizona Daily Star, St. Petersburg Times.

2 The recruitment, transportation, transfer, harboring or receipts of persons, by means of threat, or use of force or other forms of coercion, of abduction, of fraud, of deception, of the abuse of power or of a position of vulnerability or of the giving or receiving of payments or benefits to achieve the consent of a person having control over another person, for the purpose of exploitation (http://www.unodc.org/unodc/en/trafficking_human_beings.html).

REFERENCES

Ashcroft, John. 2004. *Prepared Remarks of Attorney General Ashcroft Regarding Human Trafficking*, U.S. Department of Justice, January 29, 2004. Available at (www.usdoj.gov/ag/speeches/2004/12904 aghumantrafficking.htm).

Denmore, Charles H. 2003. *Statement at Hearing on Alien Smuggling.* U.S. Senate Subcommittee on Crime, Corrections and Victims' Rights. Committee on the Judiciary, July 25. Washington, D.C., USA.

Hughes, Donna and Tatyana Denisova. 2004. "The Transnational Political Criminal Nexus of Trafficking in Women from Ukraine." In *The Prediction and Control of Organized Crime: The Experience of Post-Soviet Ukraine*, edited by J. Finckenauer and J. Schrock. New Brunswick, NJ: Transaction Publishers.

International Organization for Migration. 2003. *Data on Trafficking of Human Beings*. Data Workshop, September 8. Available at (www.iom.ch/documents/officialtxt/en/trafficking.pdf).

Lesko, Vera and Entelea Avdulaj. 2003. *The Girls and the Trafficking* The Hearth Psycho-Social Center. Albania.

Makkai, Toni. 2003. *Thematic Discussion on Trafficking in Human Beings.* 12th session of the United Nations Commission on Crime Prevention and Criminal Justice. Published by Australian Institute of Criminology [LOCATION]. Available at (www.aic.gov.au/conferences/other/makkai_toni/2003-05-traffick.pdf).

Raymond, Janice and Donna Hughes. 2001. *Sex Trafficking of Women in the United States: International and Domestic Trends*, National Institute of Justice. Washington, D.C. Available at (www.ncjrs.org/pdffiles1/nij/grants/187774.pdf).

Sellier, Homayra. 2003. "Prostitution, Paedophilia and the Trade in Human Beings." Paper presented at 1st Geneva Forum on Organized Crime, October 28, Geneva.

Stability Pact for South Eastern Europe. 2004. *Task Force on Trafficking in Human Beings*. Accessed July 7, 2004 at (www.osce. org/attf/).

Thompson, Ginger and Sandra Ochoa. 2004. "By a Back Door to the U.S.: A Migrant's Grim Sea Voyage," *The New York Times*, June 13, p.1.

Tiefenbrun, Susan. 2002. "The Saga of Susannah—A U.S. Remedy for Sex Trafficking in Women: The Victims of trafficking and Violence Protection Act of 2000." *Utah Law Review* 2002:107-175.

UNICEF. 2004. United Nations Children's Fund. *Trafficking and Sexual Exploitation*. Accessed July 7, 2004 (www.unicef.org/protection/index_exploitation.html).

United Nations. 2004. *Trafficking in Human Beings*. June 2004. Office on Drugs and Crime. Available at (www.unodc.org/unodc/en/ trafficking_human_beings.html).

_____. 2004a. *Global Programme against Trafficking in Human Beings: Analysis and Dissemination*. Office on Drugs and Crime. Accessed July 7, 2004 (www.unodc.org/unodc/en/trafficking_programme_outline.html).

U.S. Department of Justice. 2003. *Accomplishments in the Fight to Prevent Trafficking in Persons*, released by the U.S. Department of Justice, February 25, 2003 (www.usdoj.gov/opa/pr/2003/February/03_crt_110.htm).

U.S. Department of State. 2003. *Trafficking in Persons Report 2003*, Office to Monitor and Combat Trafficking in Persons, U.S. Department of State, Office for the Under Secretary for Global Affairs, June 2003 (www.state.gov/g/tip/rls/tiprpt/2003/).

U.S. Department of State. 2004. *Victims of Trafficking and Violence Protection Act of 2000: Trafficking in Persons Report*. Office to Monitor and Combat Trafficking in Persons, U.S. Department of State, Office for the Under Secretary for Global Affairs, June 2004 (www.state.gov/g/tip/rls/tiprpt/2004/).

Zhao, Gracie Ming. 2003. "Trafficking of Women for Marriage in China: Policy and Practice." *Criminal Justice* 3:83-102.

Chapter 6

MAINSTREAMING COMPARATIVE METHODOLOGY IN CRIMINAL JUSTICE/CRIMINOLOGY RESEARCH METHODS COURSES

*Rosemary Barberet**

Criminologists have made a claim for mainstreaming international/ comparative perspectives in the criminology and criminal justice curricula (Birkbeck 1993; Adler 1996; Friday 1996), but have yet to tackle a curricular issue which is at the heart of fostering international comparative research: comparative methodology. This chapter aims to isolate that gap in the curriculum, suggest ways to incorporate this topic into our teaching repertoire, and foresee the benefits that such an innovation might produce, both short and long term.

Comparative methodology is normally not taught in most criminal justice programs. In other disciplines, such as sociology and political science, comparative methodology is more likely to be taught. In criminal justice programs, its place could be in either an international criminal justice course, or in a research methods course. According to Cordner et al.

* Ramón y Cajal Research Fellow, University Carlos III de Madrid, Spain. Departamento de Ciencia Política y Sociología, Universidad Carlos III, Calle Madrid, 126, Despacho 7.24, 28903 Getafe Madrid, Spain (rbarbere@polsoc.uc3m.es).

This chapter is the result of a presentation at the 2001 annual conference of the American Society of Criminology in Atlanta. Thanks to Al Patenaude and Harry Dammer for encouraging me to publish it, to Cindy Smith and Remo Fernández for their comments as well as those of the anonymous reviewers.

(2000), only about one-third of four year undergraduate university programs in the United States have an international criminal justice course. Although there was no mention of whether these courses are mandatory or elective, it is likely that they are largely elective. Thus, introducing comparative methodology into the typical international criminal justice course would mean that only those students choosing the course, where it exists at their institution, would receive instruction in this area. In any event, the international criminal justice courses that include comparative methodology on the syllabus appear to be in the minority. As such, only a small percentage of our criminal justice students would be exposed to comparative methodology in the best of circumstances. Of the 25 syllabi in Dammer and Reichel's resource manual, *Teaching about Comparative/International Criminal Justice* (1997), only five list comparative methodology as a distinct topic for class discussion. Furthermore, the major textbooks for these courses pay little attention to comparative methodology. None of the three most popular textbooks, Fairchild and Dammer (2001), Reichel (2002) or Terrill (1999) have detailed coverage of comparative methodology. In some ways this is not all that surprising, because the textbooks are not geared as methods books but rather as texts that describe and analyse the features of non-U.S. criminal justice systems.

However, criminal justice research methods courses also fail to discuss comparative methodology. In fact, Sever's 2001 review of criminal justice research methods texts did not even select comparative methodology as a feature to examine, and his survey of 36 graduate research methods instructors also did not include any questioning regarding comparative methodology. As for the textbook coverage, among criminal justice research texts, only Neuman and Wiegand (2000) and Neuman, Wiegand, and Winterdyk (2004) have a distinct chapter on comparative methodology.

This topic is frequently covered in political science and sociology course texts. The American Sociological Association publishes a teaching resource guide for historical/comparative approaches, and there is also some evidence that in other national contexts, it is more likely to be found. Guppy and Arai's (1994) comparison of undergraduate sociology curricula in the United States and English speaking Canada revealed that 13 percent of departments in English speaking Canada offered at least one course in Comparative/Historical Methodology, compared to 6 percent in the United States (1994:223).

The result of this gap can be seen as the entrenchment of parochial criminal justice programs in the United States. Students who might be potential comparative researchers are not being exposed to the methodological material they need to conceptualise comparative research. In fact, they are not even being exposed to the possibility of thinking about engaging in such research. Given that comparative research is generally more complex than monocultural research, this means that as scholars, we are neglecting to encourage involvement in this area by students who are at the early stages of their careers, thus diminishing the productivity in international/comparative research. Bennett (2004:16) alludes to this strategy of mainstreaming international topics into the criminal justice curriculum in his 2003 Presidential Address to the Academy of Criminal Justice Sciences.

The question, then is: If we *were* to change our research methods syllabi to foster a comparative mode of thinking, what might this change entail?

Making Time and Space for Time and Space

Most American criminal justice research methods syllabi have a tendency to be data-centered and skills-based. This occurs at both the undergraduate and graduate level. They are data-centered in that they frequently embrace statistical analysis along with research methods, and they are skills-based in that students are usually given a hands-on approach to data analysis so that they can conduct their own research after the course is over. These two aspects reflect underlying assumptions in American criminology and criminal justice and mean that the broader reflections on epistemology, on the research question, and on what concerns us here—the possibility of locating the research question in *time* and *space*, usually cannot be squeezed into the research methods course. Therefore, to some extent, mainstreaming comparative methodology into the criminal justice research methods curriculum means either blending the topic into the entire syllabus, or restructuring our methods courses so that there is more of an opportunity to discuss comparative methodology as a distinct topic. Both options will be discussed in this chapter.

Sensitization

Were we to mainstream comparative methodology into our criminal justice research methods courses, the most important lesson to teach our students is to be sensitive towards the prospect of cross-cultural comparison. It is important, on the one hand, to make students aware of the world outside the United States from which there is much to learn—and to the cultural differences that exist within the United States. It is also important, on the other hand, to make them aware that intellectual tourism is only part of the point of comparative research. Students must be made aware of their own ethnocentrism, and the hegemony of Anglo-American criminological thought. In introductory sociology classes, students frequently read Horace Miner's "Body Ritual Among the Nacirema" (1956). This exercise forces them to look at their own culture from an outsider's point of view (Nacirema is American spelled backwards). Schopmeyer and Fisher (1993) go a step further in asking students to describe a feature of American culture in outsider's terms. Mitchell (1995) paired international students with native students at Oregon State University and asked them to exchange information about North American culture. These are all exercises that can be used in a criminology or criminal justice research class. Lessons learned will illustrate the bias of ethnocentrism and the importance of perspective. Certainly, many students are themselves immigrants or visitors; this richness of perspective can help the classroom experience by what David Nelken in his lifework calls the role of the "observant participant" and the "insider-outsider" (Cao and Winterdyk 2004). Methods courses must be linked to theory courses, and a discussion of the implicit ethnocentrism in many criminological theories must occur (Birkbeck 1993); students should be reminded of the importance of biography and history in the formulation of theory. Finally, there is a need for a discussion of the organization of the discipline of criminology in different cultural contexts and of the various ways of and reasons for doing research and producing knowledge.

A discussion of attitudes towards comparative research is another helpful way to start off the methods course; it also is appropriate in discussions of field research or ethnographic research. Øyen (1990:5-6) discusses "purists," "ignorants," "totalists" and "comparativists." Purists are those researchers who believe that comparative, cross-national research is no different from any other kind of research; this type of research is simply multi-level research, and no special methodological discussion is needed. "Ignorants" are those who "pursue their ideas and data across national boundaries without ever giving a thought to the possibility that such comparisons may add to the complexity in interpreting the results of the study." "Totalists" are those researchers who are acutely aware of the challenges of cross-national research, but who ignore the research problems posed by the non-equivalence of concepts and the presence of unknown variables in an unknown context. If the "totalists" were to acknowledge these problems, they would be paralysed and unable to continue this kind of research. (As such, "totalists" for Øyen are resigned relativists.) The final group are "comparativists." "Comparativists" are aware of the views of "purists" and "totalists" but believe that if the field of comparative research is to move forward, it is important to discuss and raise issues about the unique nature of doing comparative research.

Searching for Uniformity or Difference

Good training in comparative research methods is dependent on the instructor's staying in touch with the comparative methods research community in the social sciences. In criminology and criminal justice, there is a current trend towards searching for uniformity at the expense of searching for difference. There has also been a dearth of research on globalization, policy transfer across cultures (but see Newburn and Sparks 2004), and transnational and international criminal justice.

Students must be taught that searching for uniformity—patterns and trends across cultures—is only one way of conducting comparative research. Furthermore, in an era of globalization, patterns and trends may not reflect cultural similarities but rather a third influence, that of globalization. Sztompka (1990) advocates a new "search for uniqueness among increasing uniformity." He is referring to the uniformity that is a result of globalization. In this climate of uniformity, it becomes increasingly important to research any remaining differences. For Sztompka, it is important to research "cultural enclaves" by using the case study method. This methodological discussion sits well with the general discussion of the value of qualitative and quantitative research, because in comparative research, there is a historical tension between those who favor each (see Przeworski and Teune 1970; Smelser 1976). Scholars such as Ragin (1987) are working to reconcile the two worlds in an effort to provide more meaningful comparative research. The implication for our methods courses is that the case study method, so often overlooked or glossed over, is of importance for future cross-national researchers.

Conducting Research That Travels Well

Any research methods course pays a great deal of attention to the skills needed to conduct research. These skills are necessary for comparative research. Here we need to pay heed to the "process" as well as to "result" (Nelken 2000) in comparative inquiry. Not only should specific skills be highlighted, but students should be taught that the methodological discussion has value in and of itself. Often, comparative research articles in criminal justice and criminology skate over these types of discussions and the reader never gets a sense of the problems and limitations involved in this kind of research. These problems relate to data access availability and to the broader issues of validity and reliability.

First of all, American students are data-spoiled. Compared to many other nations, the United States is transparent and plentiful in its supply of data to social scientists. Students need to be challenged to think of ways to obtain access to data, or to collect data, in countries where this may not be the case. Role-playing, where students are asked to present their need for data with public agencies, or measurement exercises where students must "start from scratch" in operationalizing a concept, are useful activities in this regard. Similarly, sampling strategies should be widely discussed and adapted to cultural situations in which no population lists are available (e.g., streets with no numbers, as in some favelas in Brazil) and where sampling must be approached creatively to avoid bias. May (2001:214) refers to this issue generally as "appropriateness." Research methods must be culturally feasible, significant, and acceptable in the country studied in order to ensure validity.

Conceptual equivalence and appropriateness is another area for discussion in the part of the course that deals with measurement: can societal meanings and criminological concepts be compared? What is the meaning of bicycle theft in the Netherlands? Are gangs really the same phenomenon all over the world? A related question is why such different definitions for crime exist in the first place, how crime definitions have evolved throughout history, and the causes thereof. This discussion is of merit in international research, but it is also useful in understanding differences between States in the United States.

One of the most neglected issues in comparative criminology and criminal justice is the role of language in research methods. Other social sciences, such as anthropology, have paid greater attention to this factor (see Rubel and Rosman 2003). To date, language programs in criminal justice have been introduced mainly for the practitioner's perspective (see Crank and Loughrin-Sacco 2001). Foreign language requirements for criminology and criminal justice students are lacking in the United States. But given that many students are bilingual, addressing linguistic issues is an increasingly feasible task, besides being crucial for the good conceptualization of cross-national research. Birbili (2001) covers many of the linguistic dilemmas facing social scientists: ensuring the quality of translation, gaining conceptual equivalence, the comparability of grammatical forms, making research participants' words understandable, using translators and interpreters, and techniques for dealing with translation-related problems. Most importantly, she argues that translation-related decisions must be made explicit in comparative research articles.

Benefits

The benefits of comparative research are many and are usually very well explained in international criminology or criminal justice texts. Students are likely to see the benefits themselves once comparative research methods have been mainstreamed into their methods courses. For example, May (2001:208-210) discusses the import-mirror view, which means that by studying practices in another culture we learn more about the basis of our own; the difference view, whereby we learn from similarities as well as differences; the theory development view, whereby we test theories in a variety of cultural settings and thus aid in theory refinement; and the foresight view, whereby we can predict the viability of policy transfer by learning from another country's experience. Similarly, Bennett (2004:8-10) outlines three benefits that are specific to criminal justice: an understanding of transnational crime helps us control or reduce it; an understanding of comparative criminal justice helps us develop worldwide "best practices" as well as develop important linkages among countries' criminal justice systems; finally, comparative research helps us examine variables that have limited variation within a single nation.

Rectifying Bias in Comparative Research Productivity

The goal of mainstreaming comparative research methods into criminal justice methods courses is to expand students' horizons and encourage them to conduct comparative research. This responds to a relative lack of comparative research in general. It is also important to consider that there are kinds of comparative research in criminal justice that are less prevalent than others, at least in the US-based literature. A content analysis of presentations at the American Society of Criminology meetings in 1991, 1993, 1995, 1997, and 1999 (Barberet 2000) suggests that comparative research involving two or more countries only occurred in 5.8 percent of all presentations (see Figure 1). For the other presentations involving one country which comprise 11.5 percent of the total—some of which may be implicitly comparative—"easier" countries prevail such as western Europe (5.6 percent). It is thus doubly important that in methods classes we push students towards comparative research in parts of the world we know less about, at least in the Anglo-American literature.

The same presentations were also analysed by topical area. Figure 2 examines the proportions of U.S.-based research (e.g., monocultural), international research (research conducted in one foreign country) and comparative research (research conducted in two or more foreign countries) that are devoted to seven topic areas: theories, methods, criminal justice, law and policy, crime, criminals and victims, and academia. Comparative research is proportionately more voluminous than U.S.-based research in the areas of law and policy and crime, but less so in theories, methods, criminal justice, criminals and victims, and academia.

Thus, if we were to rectify bias in research productivity, at this juncture we should be encouraging students to tackle under-researched areas of the world—an issue which relates back to foreign language training—as well as tackling research in areas where comparative research is less common.

The Frugal Gourmet

Perhaps the most frustrating part of promulgating comparative international criminology is the counterargument that such an endeavor is a "luxury." Colleagues frequently maintain that a sabbatical abroad is not "feasible" or "realistic," that doing comparative research is "icing on the cake" or that teaching in this arena would mean neglecting the basics. Nevertheless, good

Figure 1. Countries under Study: ASC Presentations of Comparative Research 1991-1999

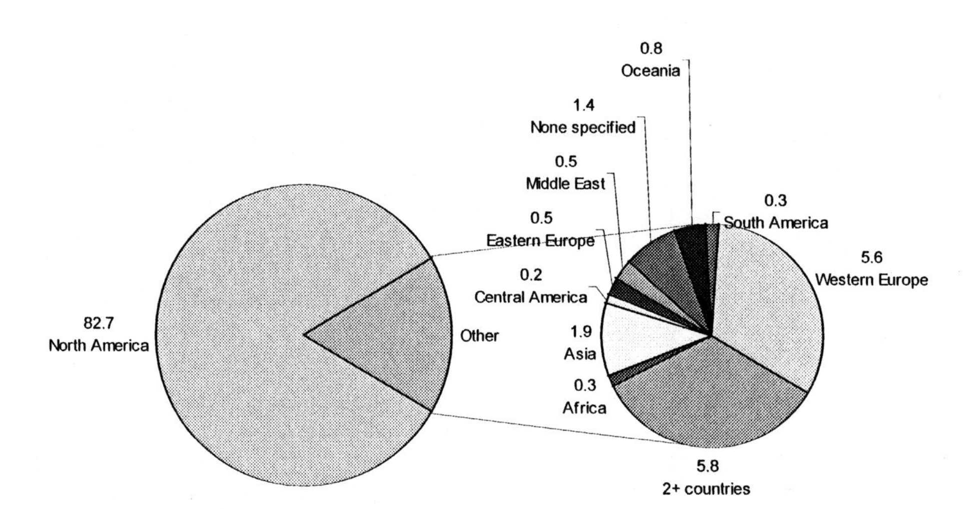

comparative research—albeit not all comparative research—can be done in imaginative ways that do not necessarily require travel, time, language skills or generous grants. Thanks to improvements in global communication, it is now routine to meet, solicit funding, conduct research, and write-up reports with colleagues around the globe. In parts of the world, funding is often even contingent on a comparative perspective. For example, European Commission grants seek "added European value," that is, the possibility that through a comparative research project, the findings may hold for more than one country. To meet the demand for comparative research, there must be inexpensive ways to "travel."

Some of these ways of conducting frugal comparative international research have to do with looking for partners. The International Center of the National Institute of Justice, conscious that the search for international research partners is key to getting comparative research off the ground, has commissioned a feasibility project in this area. With a good partner, travel is unnecessary, or at least reduced to a minimum. Research partnership and co-authorship are valuable skills to teach in a methods class even if comparative research is not being featured.

Colleagues in an international research team agree on the methodology, and each conducts the research in the country where s/he is based that s/he knows well. Findings are shared among all team members, a division of labor for analyses occurs, files cross oceans electronically, and an

Figure 2. Paper focus by topic, ASC presentations 1991-1999

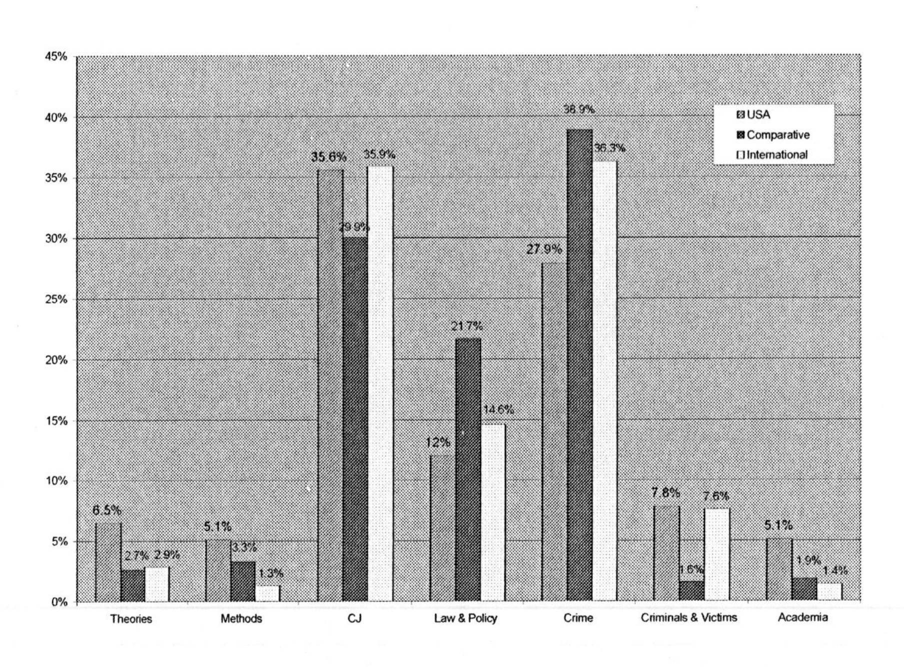

edited volume of results is produced. These types of projects are not always so straightforward. Misunderstandings occur, some players may dominate others, rights to the data may be vague, ethical issues may not be spelled out clearly enough and the methods chosen may not be appropriate in every cultural context if partners do not communicate well. However, with good communication, there is no need for expensive grants, extensive language skills or heavy travel budgets. Students in methods courses these days could even be matched with students in methods courses in other countries, and incipient training efforts in this sort of comparative exercise can occur.

Content analysis is another fruitful methodological tool for comparative research that can be done from one's armchair. Schattle (2003) describes how his students analysed media articles from around the globe for his political science course. His exercise forced students to not only look at foreign media's view of events, but foreign media's view of the United States. Besides media articles, students can be asked to conduct content analyses of a variety of sources: scholarly articles on crime; products developed by government agencies aimed at educating the public or policymakers about crime issues; websites that are crime related, such as victim assistance websites around the world; and policy documents and legislation.

Secondary analysis of cross-national datasets is yet another way to travel inexpensively. It is common in many methods courses to assign secondary data analyses as part of the workload. It would be easy to assign secondary analyses on cross-national datasets. Victimization, self-report, homicide and public opinion data, as well as many other types of data, are available for this purpose. For example, the International Crime Victims Survey is located at http://www.unodc.org/unodc/en/research_icvs_links.html, the World Health Organization Mortality database is at http://www.who.int/research/en/, and international data on criminal justice is also available from ICPSR at http://www.icpsr.umich.edu/NACJD/international_data.html. Similarly, historical analyses which cross time and space are another way for instructors to familiarise students with comparative research.

Finally, studies of migrants can serve the purpose of fostering inexpensive comparative research. The immigrant or emigrant experience is one that indirectly reflects cultural differences, and studying immigrants is an enterprise that demands little of a travel budget. Burawoy et al. (2002) stress the possibility of "going global" through an in depth series of case studies around the world. The study of migrants is similar in that it involves the study of one person or group of people that reflects multiple social forces and is a cross-cultural reflection of biography and history.

Meeting Places

Again, it is important to emphasize the importance of "meeting places" in fostering comparative research. These can be physical or virtual. If there is currently an explosion in international conferences, it is probably as a response to the increased need for meeting places and the realization that comparative international research can be done quite easily if a good research partner is found. Criminology is a fragmented discipline, especially in nations where it is still not a recognized field of study, and it is difficult to meet research partners or potential coauthors given that there is no one place to gather. It is even more difficult for students because conferences do imply physical travel. Nevertheless, it is important to encourage students to attend international conferences, or participate in the international outreach done by many national criminological societies. Again, this sort of activity is often seen as luxury. Many international societies are responding by offering substantial student discounts on registration rates, conscious that through these conferences, students embark on comparative criminological careers.

Conclusion

Comparative criminology/criminal justice courses are just a start in fostering a global competency among American criminologists. The methodological mindset of students must be changed in order to encourage comparative thinking and research. Good training in research methods can only be enhanced by raising issues dear to comparative criminologists, since these issues are central to the common themes of theory testing, validity, measurement, and analysis already contained in methods courses. Through a reform of the curriculum in these courses, criminologists can start preparing students for a future with broader horizons.

REFERENCES

Adler, Freda, ed. 1996. "Criminal Justice Education for the Global Village." *Journal of Criminal Justice Education* 7(2)(Special Issue).

Barberet, Rosemary. 2000. "The Globalization of American Criminology? A Content Analysis of ASC Presentations 1991-1999." Paper presented at the Annual Meeting of the American Society of Criminology, November 15-18, San Francisco, California.

Beirne, Piers. 1983. "Cultural Relativism and Comparative Criminology." In *Issues in Comparative Criminology*, edited by Piers Beirne and David Nelken. Aldershot: Ashgate.

Bennett, Richard R. 2004. "Comparative Criminology and Criminal Justice Research: The State of Our Knowledge." *Justice Quarterly* 21(1):1-21.

Birbili, Maria. 2001. "Translating from one Language to Another." *Social Research Update*, Issue 31. Retrieved October 28, 2003 (http://www.soc.surrey.ac.uk/sru/SRU31.html).

Birkbeck, Christopher. 1993. "Against Ethnocentrism: A Cross-Cultural Perspective on Criminal Justice Theories and Policies." *Journal of Criminal Justice Education* 4(2):307-323.

Burawoy, Michael, Joseph A. Blum, Sheba George, Zsuzsa Gille, Teresa Gowan, Lynne Haey, Maren Klawiter, Steven H.Lopez, Sean O' Riain, and Millie Thayer. 2000. *Global Ethnography: Forces,*

Connections and Imaginations in a Postmodern World. Berkeley: University of California Press.

Cao, Liqun and John Winterdyk, eds. 2004. *Lessons from International/ Comparative Criminology/Criminal Justice.* Toronto: de Sitter Publications.

Cordner, Annmarie, Harry Dammer, and Frank Horvath. 2000. "A National Survey of Comparative Criminal Justice Courses in Universities in the United States." *Journal of Criminal Justice Education* 11(2):211-223.

Crank, John P. and Steven J. Loughrin-Sacco. 2001. "Foreign Languages Across the Curriculum: A Model for the Delivery of Professional Language Training." *Journal of Criminal Justice Education* 12(1):193-211.

Crittendon, Kathleen S. 1994. "Foreigners in our Mist: Resources for Internationalizing the Sociology Major." *Teaching Sociology* 22(1):1-9.

Crow, Graham. 1997. *Comparative Sociology and Social Theory: Beyond the Three Worlds.* London: MacMillan.

Dammer, Harry R. and Philip L. Reichel, eds. 1997. *Teaching About Comparative/International Criminal Justice: A Resource Manual.* Academy of Criminal Justice Sciences.

Fairchild, Erika and Harry R. Dammer. 2001. *Comparative Criminal Justice Systems.* Belmont, CA: Wadsworth.

Friday, Paul C. 1996. "The Need to Integrate Comparative and International Criminal Justice into a Traditional Curriculum." *Journal of Criminal Justice Education* 7(2):223-239.

Guppy, Neil and Bruce A. Arai. 1994. "Teaching Sociology: Comparing Undergraduate Curricula in the United States and in English-Canada." *Teaching Sociology* 22(3):217-230.

Hantrais, Linda and Steen Mangen. 1996. *Cross-National Research Methods in the Social Sciences.* London: Pinter.

Howard, Gregory J., Graeme Newman, and William Alex Pridemore. 2000. "Theory, Method and Data in Comparative Criminology." *Criminal Justice 2000,* Volume 4. Washington, D.C.: National Institute of Justice.

May, Tim. 2001. *Social Research: Issues, Methods and Process.* Buckingham: Open University Press.

Miner, Horace. 1956. "Body Ritual Among the Nacirema." *American Anthropologist* 58:3.

Mitchell, Richard G., Jr. 1995. "International Students: Steady Hands on the Social Looking Glass." *Teaching Sociology* 23(4):396-400.

Neapolitan, Jerome. 1997. *Cross-National Crime: A Research Review and Sourcebook.* Westport, CT: Greenwood Press.

Nelken, David, ed. 2000. *Contrasting Criminal Justice: Getting from Here to There.* Aldershot: Ashgate.

Neuman, W. Lawrence and Bruce Wiegand. 2000. *Criminal Justice Research Methods: Qualitative and Quantitative Approaches.* Boston: Pearson, Allyn and Bacon.

Neuman, W. Lawrence, Bruce Wiegand, and John A. Winterdyk. 2004. *Criminal Justice Research Methods Qualitative and Quantitative Approaches: Canadian Edition.* Toronto: Pearson Education Canada.

Newburn, Tim and Richard Sparks, eds. 2004. *Criminal Justice and Political Cultures: National and International Dimensions of Crime Control.* Cullompton, Devon: Willan Publishing.

Øyen, Else, ed. 1992. *Comparative Methodology: Theory and Practice in International Social Research.* London: Sage Publications.

Pennings, Paul, Hans Keman, and Jan Kleinnijenhuis. 1999. *Doing Research in Political Science: An Introduction to Comparative Methods and Statistics.* London: Sage Publications.

Przeworski, Adam and Henry Teune. 1970. *The Logic of Comparative Social Inquiry.* New York: Wiley.

Ragin, Charles C. 1987. *The Comparative Method: Moving Beyond Qualitative and Quantitative Strategies.* Berkeley: University of California Press.

Reichel, Philip L. 2002. *Comparative Criminal Justice Systems: A Topical Approach.* Upper Saddle River, NJ: Prentice Hall.

Rubel, Paula G. and Abraham Rosman. 2003. *Translating Cultures.* Oxford: Berg.

Schattle, Hans. 2003. "Bringing Perceptions from the 'Global Village' into American Political Science Courses." *PS Political Science and Politics* 36(3):433-436.

Schopmeyer, Kim D. and Bradley J. Fisher. 1993. "Insiders and Outsiders: Exploring Ethnocentrism and Cultural Relativity in Sociology Courses." *Teaching Sociology* 21(2):148-153.

Sever, Brian. 2001. "Research Methods for Criminal Justice Graduate Students: Comparing Textbook Coverage and Classroom Instruction." *Journal of Criminal Justice Education* 12(2):337-353.

Smelser, Neil J. 1976. *Comparative Methods in the Social Sciences*. Englewood Cliffs: Prentice-Hall.

Sullivan, Christopher J. and Michael G. Maxfield. 2003. "Examining Paradigmatic Development in Criminology and Criminal Justice Courses: A Content Analysis of Research Methods Syllabi in Doctoral Programs." *Journal of Criminal Justice Education* 14(2):269-285.

Sztompka, Piotr. 1990. "Conceptual Frameworks in Comparative Inquiry: Divergent or Convergent?" In *Globalization, Knowledge and Society*, edited by Martin Albrow and Elizabeth King. London: Sage Publications.

Terrill, Richard J. 1999. *World Criminal Justice Systems: A Survey*. Cincinnati, OH: Anderson Publishing.

Vazsonyi, Alexander. 2003. "Comparative Criminology: Content or Simply Methodology?" In *Control Theories of Crime and Delinquency. Advances in Criminological Theory*, vol. 1, edited by C. Britt M.R. and Gottfredson. New Brunswick, NJ: Transaction Publishers.

Chapter 7

AMERICAN AND EUROPEAN PATHS TO INTERNATIONAL LAW ENFORCEMENT COOPERATION: MCDONALDIZATION, IMPLOSION, AND TERRORISM

*William F. McDonald**

> If the development of macro-level policing organizations in Europe, including but not limited to Interpol and Europol, has reached a modicum of harmonization, this only begs further the question of the extent to which national systems are being tuned to the same key. Addressing such questions is a task for comparative criminology... (Sheptycki 1997:134).

The Internationalization of Law Enforcement Cooperation: Two Theoretical Perspectives

In the wake of the terrorist attacks of September 11, 2001 in the United States and March 11, 2004 in Spain, the Western world is redoubling its desire for effective counter terrorism measures.[1] One key focus has been to increase cooperation among law enforcement agencies and intelligence services of different states. Terrorism has spurred such efforts in the past but does not account for the development of the institutions of international law enforcement cooperation. Those developments have been underway since the early nineteenth century in Europe and America. In describing and explaining them scholars have broadened the scope of tradi-

* Department of Sociology and Anthropology, and Institute of Criminal Law and Procedure, Georgetown University, Washington, D.C. 20057-1037 U.S.A. (wfm3@georgetown.edu).

tional comparative criminology (Nadelmann 1993; Fijnaut 1993; Fijnaut and Marx 1995; Anderson and den Boer 1994; Sheptycki 1995; McDonald 1997; Benyon 1997; Deflem 2002b).

This chapter describes the development of international law enforcement cooperation in the western world. It employs an historical and comparative approach, contrasting the paths taken by Europe[2] and America. It also examines these developments in relation to the impact of terrorism. Using the September 11th attack as a case study, it explores the extent to which the attack represented a failure of international cooperation as opposed to other kinds of failures.

While there are similarities in the trajectories of the European and American paths to international police cooperation, we argue that the continental European path reveals a stronger top-down influence whereas the American path has been shaped more by rationalizing initiatives from the bottom up. This thesis modifies but does not contradict Deflem's (2002a:21) argument that the development of international police cooperation depends in all cases upon national police institutions achieving independence from their political centers.

While it is true that bureaucratic autonomy allowed police in both places to seek international cooperation on their own initiative, political elites have played a more active role in continental European developments than in the United States. Even after the federal government in the United States assumed the key role in negotiating cooperative agreements with other states regarding law enforcement cooperation, local law enforcement agencies have developed parallel international systems of cooperation such as the Law Enforcement Intelligence Unit (Loschiavo 1975) as well as more limited binational arrangements along the Mexican and Canadian borders (McDonald 1999).

Local American police have even begun on their own to integrate many of the electronic databases of several jurisdictions, linking together not just the databases on arrests but all other public safety, criminal, and justice databases in those states (Hsu 2003; O'Harrow Jr. 2003).[3] Eventually these kinds of integrated systems are likely to become linked to similar systems in other countries, as has already happened on a limited scale between the United States and Canadian police forces (MAGLOCEN 1996).

McDonaldization

We set our analysis within two conceptual frameworks. First, we view policing and its internationalization as a manifestation of societal rationalization as described by Max Weber (1976). For Weber, modern societies have moved towards ever increasing reliance upon principles of efficiency in organizing social action. Organization on bureaucratic principles is the fundamental model for achieving this and can be pushed to extremes. The latter is illustrated, according to George Ritzer (2000; 2003), by the fast-food chain, McDonalds—where efficiency, calculability, predictability, and control through nonhuman technology dominate the social activity. Ritzer argues that more and more sectors of modern life are being "McDonaldized" (i.e., organized according to these principles). Scholars have applied this perspective to criminal justice but not yet to the internationalization of policing (Shichor 1997; McMahon 1997; Robinson 2003).

Efficiency refers to the use of the optimum method of achieving some goal. For the police, with respect to preventing harm from individuals who cross jurisdictional borders and bringing them to justice when they succeed, one key to efficiency has been the exchange of information about the wanted individuals. The technology for this has evolved from simple wanted posters and telegraphed descriptions to fingerprints, photographs, and high-speed electronic databases of criminal records and biometric measures. Efficiency is also the reason why the police preferred to kidnap fugitives who have fled to foreign countries rather than rely upon the foreign governments to cooperate (Eaton 1993).

Indeed, the reason for replacing the cumbersome nineteenth century system for obtaining cooperation between states in criminal justice matters was to improve efficiency. Formerly "letters rogatory" had be to sent from the justice ministry to the foreign ministry of the requesting state to be transferred to the foreign ministry and then the justice ministry and then local police of the receiving state. The new international agreements regarding mutual assistance in criminal matters allow for direct communication between the law enforcement agencies of different states (United Nations 1990). However, there are trade-offs between efficiency and trust. Police agencies that can afford it prefer to use less efficient but more reliable and flexible means in critical situations. They would prefer, for example, to use their own liaison officer stationed abroad to verify information rather than rely upon Interpol.

Predictability refers to the expectation that products and services will be the same over time and in all locales. The increasing international police cooperation has been accompanied by the standardization of laws, practices, and certain aspects of technology such as information systems. The standardization of laws, referred to as "harmonization," was necessary for the same act to be defined in the same way in different jurisdictions. Some investigative techniques developed in one state required adjustments in the laws and practices in other states to which they were transplanted, such as the American use of "controlled deliveries" (of drugs).

Nadelmann (1993) reports that when American DEA agents first began cooperating with European agents in investigations of drug trafficking, the American practice of allowing a consignment of drugs to go forward under control and surveillance was ineffective. Under the legality principle the European agents were required to seize illegal drugs as soon as coming into contact with them. Consequently only low-level drug couriers were being arrested. Eventually, the Americans convinced the Europeans to legalize the practice.

Calculability refers to the emphasis on the quantitative rather than the qualitative aspects of products (portion, size, cost) and services (speed of delivery). It is not evident that calculability is a feature of the international cooperation among police. It is true that costs and speed are considerations in police thinking about pursuing international fugitives and trying to prevent international crime. They do think in terms of "bigger is better"—meaning that it is better to bring down a big fish than a little one. But it is not clear that such quantitative allusions are at the expense of quality. After all, busting the mob or thwarting a terrorist are high value targets. International cooperation efforts are usually reserved for the most serious crimes/criminals. The Los Angeles Police Department, for example, established its Foreign Prosecution Unit when it was discovered that Mexican nationals—all of whom were assumed to have fled to Mexico—accounted for 100 of its 227 outstanding murder warrants (Gates and Ross 1990). If LAPD wanted numbers for their own sake, they would not have withdrawn from the business of arresting illegal aliens (McDonnell 1996).

Control through nonhuman technology refers to the ways in which the patrons as well as the employees of McDonaldized organizations have their behavior, gaze, and experience controlled, such as through limited menus, uncomfortable seating, and preprogrammed cash registers. This aspect of McDonaldization has not spread very far into the institutionalized forms of international police cooperation. Some parts of the process have been standardized, such as the universal arrest warrant form and the request for assistance that comes from the foreign country to the National Central Bureaus of INTERPOL. But the associated investigative process remains in the hands of the officers responding to the requests.

Implosions and the New Law Enforcement Space

Additionally, we view the internationalization of policing as a manifestation of a parallel social process described by postmodern theorist, Jean Baudrillard (1983), as "implosion." This refers to the disintegration or disappearance of boundaries so that formerly distinct entities collapse in on each other. Airports become shopping malls; shopping malls become theme parks, and so on. As the internationalization of law enforcement moves forward, legal implosions are happening.

It is not just political and economic borders but also legal, cultural, organizational, operational and instrumental boundaries that are disintegrating. Traditional distinctions are blurring; missions are overlapping; and identities, loyalties, and values are changing. The clearest examples are in Europe where border controls have been removed creating a single economic market. With that has come many after-implosions: the beginning of the development of a European identity among citizens of the member states (Anderson et al. 2000b); movement towards the creation of a "judicial space" within which European criminal justice systems can operate seamlessly across borders; the conflation of immigration control with crime control (Fischer 2002; Statewatch 2002e); the convergence of counter-terrorism strategy with anti-organized-crime strategies; and the blurring of internal affairs and external affairs hence the merging of "high policing" with "low policing" (Brodeur 1983) and intelligence with criminal prosecution.

This last example is well demonstrated by the removal of the "firewall" between the FBI and the CIA (Diamond 2002; Collins 2004). The wall was created and reinforced in order to prevent the use of intelligence as the basis for criminal prosecutions. Attorney General Ashcroft testified that it was the "single greatest structural cause for the September 11th problem" (*Washington Post* 2004).

The difference between law enforcement and intelligence services used to be that law enforcement's objective was to successfully prosecute a case (Berkowitz 2003). This meant gathering evidence lawfully and protecting its chain of custody so as to be able to get a conviction. In contrast intelligence services had no concern with convictions. Their purpose was to gather information that would reveal their enemy's intentions. Their purpose was to prevent actions harmful to the state's interest. Today the FBI has redefined its primary purpose with regard to terrorism as prevention, not prosecution (National Commission on Terrorism 2004).

Operationally the missions of criminal investigation organizations like the Federal Bureau of Investigation and intelligence organizations like the Central Intelligence Agency were already becoming blurred before September 11th and became more so with the passage of the U.S. Patriot Act (Lichtblau and Liptak 2003). Since the collapse of the Soviet Union the FBI has grown its overseas presence from a few liaison officers to a major presence in 40 countries. In five years the FBI had over 500 joint investigations with Russian law enforcement officials alone (McGillis 1996; Vise 2000).

Joint law enforcement operations as well as the co-location of foreign law enforcement agents in host countries are veritable mini-United Nations, models of the future of policing in the ever-shrinking globe.[4] Operating according to an unscripted mix of formal and informal understandings, and often communicating in a non-native common language (often English), and working with different concepts of legality and proper investigative technique, these officials perform their tasks in a political-legal-cultural space that resembles a node on the Internet. It is a contingent center surrounded by a web of links to different traditions, interests and loyalties.[5]

Liberal states have traditionally set limits on the geographic and substantive authority of law enforcement, judicial, and other government agencies by legal definition. Those boundaries are intended as checks on government authority. Their unintended consequence has been to prevent law enforcement agencies from effectively dealing with crime problems that cross those boundaries. The move to international law enforcement cooperation involves finding ways to implode those borders (Statewatch 2002a).[6]

Since the Treaty of Westphalia (1648) the most fundamental boundary of all in the modern nation-state is expressed in the concept of sovereignty, the demarcation of the power of the state. Max Weber identified an essential element of that concept as the exclusive authority to use force. That border also is disintegrating; or, more correctly, the traditional understanding of sovereignty is disappearing. Law enforcement and judicial cooperation and immigration control are corrosive of old conceptions of sovereignty (Camilleri and Falk 1992; Jacobson 1996; Sassen 1996; Pratt and Brown 2000).

Methodology

This chapter is based upon interviews with officials experienced in international law enforcement cooperation, plus a literature review and an analysis of open sources regarding the attacks of September 11th. Access to additional data was denied. My experience on this and another international criminal justice project suggests that the free and open access to criminal justice information, settings and people to which many criminological researchers have grown accustomed is not yet equally available in all countries including the United States regarding certain topics.

The policy-makers who are creating these international institutions and the practitioners who run them do not think that research and documentation are a valuable part of the process. They create institutions and expend enormous sums without imagining that in the future there will be need to understand what was done, why, and whether it succeeded.[7]

The Impact of Terrorism and September 11th

Terrorism has spurred progress towards greater cooperation after specific events. The 1972 massacre of the Israeli athletes at the Munich Olympic Games led to the formation of the TREVI Group for counter-terrorist cooperation among European Community member states. Yet it has also been the source of serious friction among states (Bigo 1994; Anderson and den Boer 1994). The problem is the lack of a common definition of terrorism. States agree to cooperate in general but there have been several striking refusals in particular cases. The ambiguity of the concept of terrorism provides room to justify their reticence (Anderson 2000a).

In the aftermath of the September 11th attacks some of the successes in the field of international cooperation came to light. There were heartening reports of specific instances of cooperation and common cause among law enforcement agencies in the United States, Canada, France, Germany, the United Kingdom, Spain, Italy, Jordan, the Netherlands, Pakistan, and the Philippines (Eggen 2002d; Guardian 2002; Williams 2002; Schmidt and Eggen 2002). There was also a redoubling of efforts within and between states to securitize against terrorism.

The American Response

The Failures of September 11th

The American investigations into how September 11th happened have found that it was the failure of cooperation within and among the agencies (the FBI, the CIA, the Immigration and Naturalization Service and the State Department) of the United States rather than a failure of cooperation among states that allowed the terrorists' plot to succeed (Lee and Smith 2001; Sheridan 2001; Miller 2002; Ross 2002; Kurtz 2002; Johnston 2002; Eggen 2002c; Eggen and Miller 2002; Camarota 2002; Loeb 2002; Will 2001; United States Congress 2002). Several missed opportunities were dishearteningly close-calls and point to organizational culture or legal restrictions as obstacles that prevented authorities from probably foiling the attacks (Eggen 2002a; *Washington Post* 2002b; Gerth 2003).

–Nine of the hijackers who seized the jetliners on September 11 were singled out for extra security screening at the airports that morning. Two were selected because of irregularities in their identification documents; six were chosen by a computerized screening system that resulted in a sweep of their checked baggage for weapons. The ninth was listed on travel documents as accompanying one of the other hijackers with questionable identification (Eggen 2002b). Carrying box cutters on an aircraft was not prohibited at the time.

–On August 29, 2001 a desperate FBI agent pleaded with his superiors to begin an aggressive search for Khalid al-Mihdhar, who two weeks later helped commandeer the plane that was crashed into the Pentagon. The lawyers in the FBI's National Security Law Unit refused his request because the agent's information had come through intelligence channels which legally could not be used for criminal investigations—the legal firewall between the CIA and the FBI. The agent responded with a scathing email:

"Someday someone will die and (legal) wall or not–the public will not understand why we were not more effective and throwing every resource we had at certain 'problems.' Let's hope the National Security Law Unit will stand behind their decisions then, especially since the biggest threat to us now, [Osama bin Laden], is getting the most 'protection'" (Eggen and Priest 2002).

Al-Mihdhar and fellow Flight 77 hijacker, Nawaf al-Hamzi, attended a meeting of Al Qaeda operatives in Kuala Lumpur in January 2000. Malaysian authorities provided the CIA with information about the meeting and the two men (Isikoff 2002). The CIA knew that al-Mihdahar held a visa that allowed him multiple reentries into the United States. The CIA counter-terrorism unit continued to monitor al-Mihdhar and al-Hamzi but neglected to put them on the "watch-list" (Gerth 2003). According to Eleanor Hill, staff director of the Joint Congressional inquiry into September 11th, "There were numerous opportunities during the tracking of these two terrorists when the CIA could have alerted the FBI and other law enforcement authorities to the probability that these individuals either were or would be soon in the United States" (Eggen and Priest 2002). That was not done until August 23, 2001. When the CIA finally requested the State Department to add al-Mihdhar and al-Hamzi to its watchlist, the INS and the U.S. Customs Service discovered that they were already in the country. FBI headquarters was notified and issued an order to its Los Angeles field office to search for them. The Los Angeles office received the order on September 11th as the two men were commandeering American Airlines Flight 77 to crash it into the Pentagon (United States Congress 2002).

The INS and the FAA have testified that if the CIA had made clear to them the urgency of the threat posed by al-Mihdhar and al-Hamzi they might have been able to apprehend them. The FAA would have entered their names on a list that would have picked them up in the reservation process. Both men used their own names when they bought tickets for the American flight. United States intelligence officials disputed this account saying that the CIA's August 23rd notice was marked "immediate" and had warned, "We recommend that these two individuals be watch-listed immediately to be denied entry into the United States" (*Washington Post* 2002b). Meanwhile the FBI had an undercover source who was friendly with al-Mihdhar and al-Hamzi in San Diego and reporting on them to the FBI. But, the FBI agent handling the case did not ask the source for their names and did not know what he had.

–A July 10th (2001) memo to headquarters from Phoenix FBI agent, Kenneth Williams, warned that followers of Osama bin Laden might be taking flying lessons in the United States. The memo was not acted upon or circulated or shared with other intelligence agencies.[8]

–On August 16th Zacarias Moussaoui, the alleged "20th hijacker," was arrested by the FBI in Minnesota after he aroused suspicion at a flight school. The FBI learned from French intelligence that Moussaoui had radical Islamic ties. They knew he had requested to train on a flight simulator for a 747 trip from London's Heathrow to New York's JFK. They were absolutely convinced that he wanted to do something with the large aircraft and speculated that he wanted to crash it into the World Trade Center (Isikoff 2002; Johnston 2002).

The Minnesota field office requested permission from headquarters to obtain a warrant to search Moussaoui's computer—later found to contain detailed information about jetliners, wind patterns, and crop-dusting aircrafts. Headquarters fiercely opposed the application for the warrant because they lacked sufficient information to show that he was acting as an agent of a foreign power, which was necessary to obtain a warrant under the Foreign Intelligence Surveillance Act. Headquarters even considered deporting Moussaoui and his computer to France where more permissive law would have allowed the French police to search it. Meanwhile, headquarters never mentioned to the Minnesota office anything about the Phoenix memo regarding terrorists seeking aviation training. It may have provided the evidentiary support needed for the search warrant (Eggen 2002a; Miller and Eggen 2002; United States Congress 2002:21).

–All 19 suspected hijackers involved with the September 11th attacks had obtained visas from American consulates. None triggered any alarms in the State Department's database of inadmissible foreigners (Sheridan 2001). An analysis by experts of the visa-application forms of 15 of the 19 hijackers (whose forms were obtainable) concluded that if the State Department had simply followed the law all 15 visas should have been denied because they lacked validity on their face. They omitted required information (Mowbrary 2002).

–In August 1998 the Intelligence Community learned that a group of unidentified Arabs planned to fly an explosive-filled plane from a foreign country into the World Trade Center. The information was passed to the FBI and the Federal Aviation Administration (FAA). The FAA found the plot highly implausible because of the state of that country's aviation program. Additionally, they thought that a flight originating outside the United States would be detected before it reached its target inside the country. The FBI took no action on the information (United States Congress 2002:27).

–In October 1998 the FAA told airlines to be on a "high degree of alertness" against possible hijackings by followers of Osama bin Laden. The warning was based on statements made by bin Laden after U.S. attacks on suspected Al Qaeda locations in Afghanistan and Sudan in August 1998. The circulars did not order the airlines to increase security. Between January 2001 and August 2001 the FAA issued 15 security advisories. The April 18th circular warned that Middle Eastern terrorists might try to hijack or blow up a U.S. plane. It urged airlines to "demonstrate a high degree of alertness" (Salant 2002).

–On January 6, 1995 one week before the Pope's visit to the Philippines, Abdul Hakim Murad was arrested by Manila police after he accidentally set off a fire alarm in his apartment located close to the pope's route. He had been mixing materials to make bombs. His apartment was a virtual bomb factory with gallons of sulfuric acid, nitric acid, glycerin, beakers and kettles, and detonating devices, plus stacks of passports for various countries. Under torture by Philippine intelligence he revealed a plan which bin Laden operatives referred to as "Bojinka"—"loud bang." After assassinating the Pope the plan called for bombing 11 U.S. airliners simultaneously and flying an airplane into the CIA headquarters in Langley, Va. (Struck et al. 2001).

The plan was detailed and well financed. Philippine intelligence compiled extensive information including: the precise flights to be targeted—United 808, Delta 59, Northwest 6, and others; the calculations as to when to detonate the bomb on each flight; the names of dozens of people involved; a list of aviation schools where Murad trained as a pilot; an account of how the financing moved through a banking firm; and the names of Murad's two roommates: Ramzi Ahmed Yousef and Wali Khan Amin Shah (Struck et al. 2001).

Murad and the information were turned over to the United States. In 1997, Murad, Yousef, and Shah were convicted for their participation in the 1993 bombing of the World Trade Center. But evidently the plan was never abandoned. After September 11th, former Gen. Renado S. De Villa, who was head of the security effort for the pope's visit to the Philippines said, "Murad clearly indicated it was a large-scale operation. They were targeting the U.S.; and they had a worldwide network. It was very clear they continued to work on that plan until someone gave the signal to go." When the attacks in New York and Washington were broadcast on television, a Philippine investigator exclaimed, "It's Bojinka!" Later he said: "We told the Americans everything about Bojinka. Why didn't they pay attention?" (Struck et al. 2001).

Reshuffling the Security Institutions

At the national level the Bush administration is trying to solve these various failures by reorganizing many of the agencies with remits related to counter-terrorism into the massive new Department of Homeland Security and by integrating more closely intelligence activities with criminal investigative activities and federal with local law enforcement (McGee 2002; Clymer 2001; Gugliotta and Krim 2001).[9]

Critics are skeptical about whether the reorganization will result in a net gain. Neither the CIA nor the FBI are included in the new Department of Homeland Security. The two agencies have histories of non-cooperation and turf wars within and between them which were freshly documented in the inquiries after September 11th.[10] No amount of reorganization is going to solve the problems of risk-avoidance by career bureaucrats, of disputes over the interpretations of the laws, or of the inability to think outside traditional parameters.

In the opinion of Coleen Rowley, General Counsel of the FBI's Minnesota field office that was denied the authorization to seek a search warrant in the Moussaoui case, the fact that the careers of high-ranking FBI officials have in the past been ruined by poor decisions in high-profile cases has "resulted in a climate of fear which has chilled aggressive FBI law enforcement action/decisions" (Miller and Eggen 2002). In a scathing letter to FBI Director, Robert Muller, regarding the FBI's handing of the Moussaoui case, Rowley said the problem stems from the FBI's huge bureaucracy with numerous layers of supervisors who are afraid of making decisions that might be criticized by Congress and the public (Eggen 2002a).

The Joint Congressional intelligence panel investigating the attacks concluded that U.S. agencies were aware of the growing threat of bin

Laden's terrorist network and had ample warnings of a possible attack using airplanes but failed to reallocate resources to match the seriousness of the threat; failed to communicate among themselves; and failed to interpret the law correctly (United States Congress 2002; Priest and Eggen 2002a; Priest and Eggen 2002b; Schmidt 2002).

Following the bombings of the two American embassies in East Africa in August 1998, George Tenet, CIA Director, notified his deputies: "We must now enter a new phase in our efforts against Bin Laden...We are at war...I want no resources or people spared in this effort, either inside CIA or in the [intelligence] community" (United States Congress 2002:9). Nevertheless, there was no major reallocation of resources within the CIA to counter-terrorism until September 11. Moreover, FBI officials were not made aware of the seriousness of the assessment (Priest and Eggen 2002b; United States Congress 2002:18).

Commentators familiar with the logic of both criminal investigations and clandestine intelligence work (espionage) note that neither one is well suited to get the kind of tactical intelligence needed to prevent a terrorist attack (Loeb 2002). The intelligence community's job is to provide strategic, not tactical intelligence. There are major obstacles to providing the latter. Intelligence operatives cannot arrange quick meetings with sources or superiors. The tactical information they obtain is typically only a fragment of a larger picture and its validity cannot be established easily.

The European Response

At the level of improving international cooperation in law enforcement, the September 11th attacks brought a swift response. Nine days after the attacks the European Union's Justice and Home Affairs (JHA) Council agreed "to speed up the process of creating an area of freedom, security and justice and to step up cooperation with its partners, especially the United States" (Council of Europe 2002c). It approached Washington with a proposal to negotiate an agreement to jointly fight terrorism. The next day the United States responded calling for an agreement that would go far beyond terrorism and would cover general "criminal matters" as well (Norton-Taylor 2002; Statewatch 2002d).

In February 2002, JHA endorsed opening of secret negotiations with the United States on: "one or several agreements on cooperation in criminal matters" and to "continue the informal exploratory talks with the US side" (Statewatch 2002d). As regards "serious crime" the EU wants to "facilitate search and seizure in bank accounts" and wants to reduce delays in cooperation by creating "contact points in each Member State and in the USA" (Statewatch 2002b). The EU proposed two major initiatives: "the setting up of joint investigative teams" and "creating a common approach to searches, seizures, interception of telecommunications." The United States wants to address "narrowing down the political offense" exception (to extradition), extradition of nationals and "special courts."[11] The EU is seeking assurances that those extradited will be the subject of ordinary U.S. court proceedings (Statewatch 2002b).

A civil rights watchdog group challenged the secrecy of the negotiations but the Council allowed only partial access to the documents involved on the grounds that "the interest of protecting the Council's objectives outweighs the interest in 'democratic control'...which is referred to by the applicant" (Statewatch 2002d). In the absence of direct access to the negotiations, we extrapolate as to the contours of the future forms of cooperation from the trajectories of U.S. and European developments in the past together with our theoretical assumption of ever-increasing standardization.

Two Routes to Law Enforcement Cooperation

The American Approach: Bottom Up

Historically the construction of institutions of international law enforcement cooperation have taken different routes. In America where policing has always had a democratic character, they have been driven from the bottom up. In (continental) Europe where policing has always had the mark of authoritarian governments about it, they have come from the top down. In America, police trying to catch "bad guys" got together on their own without any support from the federal government and devised ways to respond to mobile criminals. In 1871, police executives gathered in St. Louis to develop ways to cooperate.

They considered a proposal to "provide for a systematic plan of transmitting Detective Information throughout the several States of the Union,...to adopt a system of [telegraphic] cypher for the use of police throughout the country"; to arrange for a more complete exchange among police departments of the photographs of criminals; and to establish as a permanent organization called the National Police Association which became the International Association of Chiefs of Police in 1893 after Canadian police officials began attending the meetings (Smith Jr. 1960).

They agreed to notify each other of fugitives. They adopted the new scientific methods of personal identification, first the Bertillon method and later, fingerprints. With money from their own budgets, they established a national criminal records system. It eventually became the famous FBI criminal records system but only after local police leaders persuaded Congress that it was the federal government's responsibility to maintain such a system. This was not an easy sell because Americans had always been fearful of losing their liberty. For over a century, Congress refused to establish a federal law enforcement agency. It feared the model of the European national police agencies with their spies and political intrigues (Walker 1977:47). Even before 1871, American police officers went far beyond their local jurisdictions in pursuit of criminals. Often they were supported by private financial interests such as the New England Association against Counterfeiting, a group of bank directors. They authorized Francis Tukey, head of the Boston Police Department, to pursue criminals all the way to Canada on their behalf. Founded in 1832, the mutual aid society once succeeded in getting the Canadian government to raid and capture twenty-five offenders in one operation (Lane 1971).

In 1907 when the Bolivian government appealed to the United States for help in dealing with the famous bank robbers, Butch Cassidy and the Sundance Kid, who were plying their trade down there after being run out of the country, the federal government sent a private detective agency, the Pinkertons, to the rescue. The United States did not have a federal police agency at the time. The FBI was not established until 1908. It was the Pinkertons who ran the "Wild Bunch" out of the Old West. Indeed Butch and Sundance are the paradigmatic case of the problems in dealing with cross-border criminals. Local police lacked the authority, the resources, and the motivation to pursue them. Their hide-out was located at the intersection of three states. They robbed in two and lived with impunity in the third. It was a private agency, the American Bankers Association, whose members were losing money that hired the Pinkertons to fill in the jurisdictional and motivational gaps in the law enforcement networks (Nadelmann 1993).

While at the federal level American officials did nothing to develop a system of international law enforcement cooperation, at the local level it was a different story. In 1922 (a year before the Vienna Congress at which International Criminal Police Commission (INTERPOL) was established) Richard Enright, the Commissioner of the New York City Police Department, convened a meeting of police officials to foster cooperation among police agencies. Within a year the initiative went international. Although only five foreign delegates had attended, the group established the International Police Conference (IPC) to promote international police cooperation and improve policing. The IPC failed to attract foreign officials. After a few attempts at coordination with INTERPOL, IPC's international aspirations failed to materialize (Deflem 2002b:132).

The European Approach: Top Down

Europol: Elite Answer to the New Security Needs

In Europe political elites have sought to develop international cooperative police arrangements to defend the status quo; to protect the state from political and economic subversion; and most recently, to meet the security needs of a newly integrated single economic market. Current developments appear to be driven more by the political desire to show progress in the integration of Europe than by the operational or organizational needs of national law enforcement agencies.[12]

Europol, the latest achievement of European efforts to establish an institution for international cooperative policing, was created under Title VI of the Treaty on European Union, on "Cooperation in the Fields of Justice and Home Affairs," often referred to as the "third pillar" of the European Union (EU). Included within this pillar is a bundle of issues which (Bigo 1994) preferred to as the "European internal security field": international crime; terrorism; immigration; and police, judicial and penal matters. Europol is likely to survive but some individuals see it as Chancellor Kohl's "baby" and many would prefer that it had not developed. It is not supported by many EU member states. It has not been receiving the intelligence reports from national organizations as required for its intelligence analysis. Law enforcement officials are somewhat skeptical about the EU arrangements because they are aware that the executive/administrative elites dominate JHA and these elites lack law enforcement experience and are not usually sensitive to the interests of the law enforcement community (Anderson et al. 2001:23).[13] Before September 11, the Americans had not embraced it.

It is not only with minimal police input that the major institutions of cooperation in the European internal security field have evolved. There has also been a lack of democratic governance and transparency. Neither judicial nor parliamentary bodies have exercised much scrutiny over the development or operations of the field. Critics complain about a serious "democracy deficit" and about inadequate attention to civil rights. Nevertheless the ministers in the Justice and Home Affairs Council continue to move the project steadily towards an operational law enforcement agency with even less democratic accountability (Statewatch 2002c; Statewatch 2002a).

Nineteenth Century European Initiatives

Perhaps the first European multinational gathering of police officials was the meeting in 1819 of the Central Investigation Commission created by the Bundestag of the German Confederation at the initiative of Metternich. "It's charge," writes the historian Liang (1980), "was to investigate the origin and the ramifications of the current revolutionary agitation in Germany against the constitution and the domestic peace of the Bund and of its separate states" (p.199).

The revolutions of 1848 unleashed a flood of political refugees in Europe and made police officials conscious of the need to communicate transnationally. In 1851, trying to capitalize on the opportunity provided by hosting the Great Exhibition at the Crystal Palace, the British government welcomed foreign police to the Great Exhibition by subsidizing their expenses. In return they were supposed to provide London Police Commissioner Mayne with daily intelligence reports. However no permanent cooperative arrangements resulted (Nadelmann 1992:IV-46).

In 1851, the Police Union of the German States was founded by Karl Ludwig Friedrich von Hinckeldey, Police President of Berlin. Concerned about revolutionary unrest, the ultraconservative von Hinckeldey convened a secret conference among police representatives from four German states to consider establishing a system of exchanging information about revolutionary agitators. The German Police Union was founded the next year. Von Hinckeldey was appointed by King Friedrich Wilhelm IV and saw himself as defender of the status quo. The Police Union never focused on ordinary crime. It only pursued political opponents (Deflem 2002b:49-57).

By the 1870s, the activities of anarchists, socialists, and other political opponents of conservative regimes appeared to be increasingly transnational. Central European governments responded in kind by calling for the creation of a system of international law enforcement cooperation. Calls went out after the assassination of Tsar Alexander II in 1881, and again after the assassination of French President Sadi Carnot in 1894. But it was not until the assassination of Empress Elizabeth of Austria by an Italian anarchist in1898 that a conference was held in Rome to cooperate in the suppression of anarchist violence. Fifty-four delegates from twenty-one countries attended (Nadelmann 1992:IV-27; Liang 1992).

The conference resulted in the beginnings of an international system of cooperation. The conferees agreed that all states should adopt an improvement to the Bertillonage system of identification for anarchists and criminals. They enacted the Russian proposal that states include a clause in their extradition treaties providing that attacks on heads of states or their families be made grounds for extradition. They went along with a German proposal to establish a central agency to track anarchists and to communicate directly with other central agencies. Also, they agreed that the old fashioned diplomatic channels and formal salutations would be replaced by plain talk directly among police through telephonic and telegraphic communications (Jensen 1981).

The assassination of U.S. President, William McKinley, in 1901 prompted calls for a second meeting to expand upon the achievements of the Rome conference. Two years of negotiation followed during which most European governments refused to support a proposal by the Tsar's representatives to surrender all foreign anarchists on demand. But in St. Petersburg in 1904 ten states did agree to institutionalize the cooperative arrangements developed in Rome (Jensen 1981).[14]

By the end of the century there were other international conferences calling for police cooperation. Some were initiated by moral entrepreneurs seeking to focus police attention on their particular moral concerns (to suppress traffic in "white slavery," London, 1899; "white slavery," Paris,

1904; pornography, Paris, 1910). Others were about general police matters (Buenos Aires, 1905; Madrid, 1909; Sao Paulo, 1912; and Washington, 1913) (Nepote 1977; Nadelmann 1992:IV-49).

Despite all these meetings an effective international system of cooperation remained embryonic at best. In his survey of European police systems on the eve of World War I, the American scholar Raymond Fosdick concluded:

> There has been no consistent international action [against crime] worthy of the name. To be sure, criminal records are often exchanged between nations on the basis of special treaties and a few cities cooperate in reference to certain cases or classes of cases...But of broad cooperation on a systematic basis there is none...To be sure, some of the police departments, particularly Paris and London, occasionally communicate directly with each other, leaving the diplomatic formalities to follow in their own good time, but this practice is irregular and is generally frowned upon in high places (Fosdick 1915: 333ff as cited in Nadelmann 1992: IV-50).

Interpol: Origins and Eclipse

Fosdick (1915:333ff) enumerated several standardizing features necessary for effective cooperation including an international bureau of identification, a universal extradition treaty, common police codes for international communication and a uniform system for distributing information about mobile criminals. Many of these ideas were taken up at yet another international police conference, initiated by Henri Smart, the Chief of Police of the tiny state of Monaco which relied heavily upon international cooperation. The First International Congress of Judicial Police held in Monte Carlo in April 1914 was sponsored by Prince Albert I of Monaco. Over 300 law enforcement and public officials, lawyers, and scholars attended the meeting from Europe, Persia, and four Latin American countries–Brazil, Cuba, Guatemala, and El Salvador. The conferees adopted proposals for the establishment of centralized international criminal records and for uniform extradition procedures. A follow-up conference was planned but war intervened.

As part of the post-war effort to restore order, a senior Dutch police officer, Captain M.C. van Houten, circulated a letter to several European police chiefs suggesting the establishment of an international police agency under the auspices of the League of Nations. Nothing came of it. Then in 1923 the former and future chancellor of Austria (and police commissioner of Vienna), Dr. Johann Schober, convened another international criminal police congress. Unlike the Congress in Monaco where diplomats, lawyers, and magistrates attended, most of the 131 participants in Vienna were police officials. They considered creating an international police bureau to be attached to the League of Nations. Instead they created an independent agency, the International Criminal Police Commission, eventually known as Interpol (Anderson 1989).[15] Initially one of Interpol's highest priorities was the suppression of counterfeiting—a problem well suited to the growth of an international police institution but far removed from the concerns of the victims of common crime. During World War II, Interpol was infiltrated by Nazi police and carried on under Nazi influence. Interpol was revitalized in 1946 at a gathering of earlier members of the Commission. The meeting was organized by Belgian Police Chief, F. Louwage. Once again Interpol's purpose was to help restore order but also to re-establish the organization's operational achievements from before the war (Fijnaut 1987:35; Deflem 2002b:205).

The reconstituted Interpol governed by French officials flourished into the 1970s increasing its membership to more than 100 countries. Yet it remained as a communication exchange system through which police agencies could send messages and post notices regarding particular crimes or offenders. It also served as a central repository for criminal records, receiving duplicate copies of fingerprints from contributing agencies (Fooner 1975). By the early 1970s it was ridiculed by European critics as the "Parisian letter box" for being slow, inefficient, and unresponsive to the regional needs of Europe, its main service user (80 percent of its message traffic) (Fijnaut 1987:38; Anderson and den Boer 1992). Ideas for a European alternative to Interpol began to surface.[16]

The Emergence of The European Security Field

For more than two decades proposals were advanced by police experts and politicians. Meanwhile the European States were building the infrastructure of the new European political and legal institutions that would be necessary to support a more robust form of cooperation. Eventually the recommendation of Chancellor Kohl of Germany for a supranational European law enforcement institution, a kind of FBI for Europe, prevailed.

The need for an effective supra-national European law enforcement institution became apparent in the 1970s as the result of drug trafficking and terrorism. Interpol's French officials resisted calls for reform except for a minor concession granted in 1971 when French President Pompidou decided to lead a Western European wide effort against illegal narcotic drug trafficking.[17] It was the wave of terrorist violence in the early 1970s (the Munich Olympics massacre, the Baader Mienhof gang in Germany and the Brigate Rosse in Italy) that triggered a critical decision. The ministers of internal affairs meeting as the Council of Europe in Rome in 1975 established a body it called "TREVI" whose purpose was to stimulate co-operation in the fight against terrorism (Fijnaut 1987:41; Wilkinson 1985:282).

Although TREVI's purpose was limited originally to counter-terrorism, in 1986 without explanation the TREVI-Ministers (for Justice and Home Affairs-JHA) expanded their mission into a broader fight against international crime. They chose to bypass Interpol and move towards the creation of new institutional mechanisms. In the same year the Single European Act initiated the process of creating an economic area with no internal barriers to the freedom of movement. The preceding year the Benelux countries (Belgium, France, Germany, the Netherlands, and Luxembourg) had signed the Schengen Agreement by which they formalized police cooperation amongst themselves (Benyon 1997). The Schengen agreement was seen by some as a possible blueprint for European-wide cooperation (Benyon et al. 1993:149).

The search for new cooperative police arrangements became urgent when the European Economic Community agreed to eliminate border controls among the member states in 1992 (Birch 1989; Alderson and Tupman 1990). The target date slipped several times to March 1995 but the pressure was on. At the European Council meeting in June 1991, Chancellor Kohl moved for the creation of a European Criminal Police Office which would combat international and European crime. His proposal was accepted. The idea fit with a proposal from a working group (III) of TREVI. It resulted in the Ad Hoc Working Group on Europol (Benyon 1997:115; Rupprecht 1993).

In June 1993 the TREVI ministers agreed to the establishment of the European Drug Unit (operational in February 1994) whose purpose was to analyze information on drug trafficking and facilitate the exchange of intelligence among European Union police forces and customs agencies. In November 1993 when the Treaty on European Union came into force, the TREVI Group morphed into the "third pillar" of the new European Union. Under Title VI (article K) of the treaty, the third pillar dealt with the matters of justice and home affairs which include: asylum; external border controls; immigration; anti-fraud and anti-drug efforts; judicial cooperation; and police cooperation including the establishment of a European Police Force (Europol) (Benyon 1997:113).

In July 1995 the Council of Europe drew up a convention for the establishment of a new organization called "Europol" (European Police Office). The convention entered into force on October 1, 1998 (Council of Europe 2001). Europol began as a coordinating and analytic organization with no operational authority. Officials discouraged the idea that it would become a European FBI.[18] Officially its purpose is "to improve the effectiveness of the competent authorities in the Member States and cooperation between them in an increasing number of areas: preventing and combating terrorism, unlawful drug-trafficking, trafficking in human beings, [and other international crimes]" (Council of Europe 2001).

Notwithstanding assurances to the contrary, in April 2002, JHA ministers agreed to give Europol some limited operational authority (Statewatch 2002a).[19] What is more, after two years of debate JHA established a companion European-wide prosecutorial institution called Eurojust. The EU Council Decision formally establishing the European prosecutions office was adopted on February 28, 2002 (Council of Europe 2002a). A provisional Eurojust was set-up in December 2000 and handled some 170 cases in its first year of operation. Eurojust is comprised of prosecutors (magistrates) or police and is already demonstrating that a new era in European law enforcement cooperation has arrived (Statewatch 2000; Statewatch 2001a).

Transatlantic Tensions

A month after the September 11th attacks President Bush sent a letter to the European Commission listing 40 areas of concern for improving cooperation in criminal matters (Statewatch 2002f). Some matters had to do with anti-terrorism; many did not. The latter covered criminal investigations, data surveillance, border controls, and immigration policies. The list represents a summary of most of the current tensions in the transatlantic relationship. Many of the items are new versions of old, familiar problems in the field of international law enforcement cooperation: sharing information; speedy communication; authority for direct communication between police; new telecommunications technology; and expanded extradition. The borders to be overcome are mostly legal ones: some old ones restricting extradition; others new ones created to protect data. For example, the provisions of the Europol convention on privacy and sharing of personal data are problematic for the United States (Council of Europe-JHA 1999). The convention requires that third countries not simply guarantee privacy but to do so by virtually replicating the exact same mechanisms employed by EU member states.

The convention's balance between protecting public security and the protection of personal privacy is regarded by some American officials has tipped too far in the latter direction. As the September 11th investigations have made clear, a critical ingredient in criminal investigations and the prevention of terrorist attacks is information sharing. Sometimes it must be done rapidly as fast-breaking situations unfold in real time. Other times it needs to done through the power of searching databases. The convention has posed major obstacles to such sharing. Law enforcement people wanted to create a database on stolen vehicles. The initiative was defeated because it would have required identifying the true owner of the vehicle. Law enforcement officials wanted to create a database of missing children. It failed because it would have required the permission of the missing children. The Europol Convention standards of privacy are so high that experienced law enforcement officials worry that they may force law enforcement officers to cut corners in order to meet the public demand to solve crimes. Finding a balance more favorable to public security is likely to be a focus of current negotiations and is likely to be a perennial source of tensions in the dialogue.

Until September 11th the United States had other concerns about the law enforcement implications of the evolution of the European Union. The Union's directives are somewhat vague. The national implementations of them go much further than the directives. With 25 Member States, one gets

25 different interpretations. This makes joint operations difficult. Now that the EU wants to engage in joint operations more broadly, this difference will need to be further standardized.

As Member States adopt common legal policies, the United States worries about the fate of the bilateral agreements it has with them. It took more than 20 years to establish fairly effective bilateral cooperative agreements. If they are now replaced with a multilateral agreement, one ends up with the "lowest common denominator" problem. United States will probably try to avoid multilateral and preserve its bilateral capabilities with individual states.

Before September 11th the Americans sensed that the Europeans were turning inward upon themselves. Their focus had shifted away from the trans-Atlantic space as well as from other parts of the world. In an age of globalization they seemed preoccupied with regionalization. Europol, for example, might become a successful regional institution. It already has spun off 60 percent of the work done by Interpol. But in today's world the United States needs a truly international law enforcement institution with which to ally its efforts. Major criminal and terrorist threats are coming from the Middle East, Latin America, and Asia. Another pre-September 11th tension was the difficulty American officials were having in participating in crafting new European Union policies and institutions. Their attempts to participate even in a consultative role such as commenting upon proposals were frustratingly limited. Moreover, there was a pervasive suspicion and distrust of the Americans.

One of the American complaints about their European partners is undoubtedly seen in a different light today. It was about the degree of cooperation which the Americans thought should have been better. Measured against the standard of cooperation among and within U.S. law enforcement and intelligence agencies as revealed by the investigations into the failures of September 11th, the cooperation the Americans were getting should probably have been rated as superior. Clearly this points out that cooperation is not all a matter of standardization, harmonization, and international politics. No matter how perfectly the modules of the international space station fit together mechanically, if the human groups on board have their personal reasons to compete, there will be conflict in the new law enforcement space.

For their part, the Europeans note that the United States has not signed the various conventions protecting the privacy and human rights that European states have guaranteed individuals living in the European Union. They worry that direct communication between police in urgent situations would subvert accountability. They object to the fact that the United States practices capital punishment;[20] and they disapprove of the unilateralist stance taken by the George W. Bush administration.[21]

Transatlantic Cooperation since the 1970s

Transatlantic cooperation in law enforcement did not happen to any significant degree until the 1970s. Americans did not participate in any of the early European conferences to create law enforcement cooperative mechanisms. It was not until 1923 at a conference, which resulted in the founding of Interpol, that the United States was first represented. Even then it was not attended by a federal official but by the Chief of the New York City Police Department (Nadelmann 1992:IV-52). The United States did not join Interpol until 1938, and until recently had minimal contact with it (Nadelmann 1993:92). Today Interpol's Secretary General, Ronald K. Noble, is an American who lacks operational experience as a law enforcement offical but was the Undersecretary for Enforcement, U.S. Department of Treasury, and former professor of law. Nonetheless, 75 percent of the traffic handled by the U.S. Interpol bureau are requests coming from abroad. When American law enforcement agencies run across an occasional international matter they generally refer it to the FBI rather than pursue it themselves.

The United States did not conceive of trying to fight crime abroad until recently. President Lyndon Johnson's crime commission includes numerous reports published in 1967 which describes America's crime problem and what should be done about it. It never suggested fighting crime from abroad (President's Commission on Law Enforcement and Administration of Justice 1967a). That old mind-set is gone. In 1995, President Clinton issued PDD-42, the first national security directive ever to deem international crime to be a national security threat. It directed all relevant federal agencies to join together to develop strategies to combat transnational crime. At the international level it committed the United States to building alliances with like-minded countries. The President's International Crime

Control Strategy listed eight U.S. goals and objectives against transnational crime: to extend the first line of defense beyond U.S. borders; to protect U.S. borders by attacking smuggling and smuggling-related crimes; to deny safe haven to international criminals; to counter international financial crime; to prevent criminal exploitation of international trade; to respond to emerging international crime threats; to foster international cooperation and the rule of law; and to optimize the full range of U.S. efforts (Winer 1998:67).

The new thinking that shaped the President's strategy came about as the result of experiences between the 1960s and the 1990s, which convinced American officials that such a strategy was feasible. Particularly important was the joint investigation of the Mafia with Italian officials, the "Pizza Connection" (Alexander 1988). Prior to the late 1970s the idea of working together with foreign law enforcement officials, sharing intelligence, and trusting their judgments and integrity was unimaginable. It was axiomatic that foreign officials, especially from countries known for organized crime and corruption, could not be trusted. They might either reveal information corruptly or use it to make a "first strike" arrest, grabbing the headlines and terminating the investigation.

That old verity crumbled when an American prosecutor named Louis Freeh and an Italian magistrate named Giovanni Falcone began tripping over each other's investigations of a common enemy. The Sicilian La Cosa Nostra had taken control of heroin trafficking from the French and had created a worldwide narcotics trafficking and money laundering center in Sicily. Both U.S. and Italian law enforcement authorities were investigating the same group. Several cases had been made by each country. The two nations were competing for defendants and jurisdictional control (Martin 1998; Martin 1990-1991).

Finally, Freeh and Falcone sat down together and got past some cultural blinders. They both had some surprises. Not all Italian magistrates are corrupt and untrustworthy; and not all American prosecutors are arrogant fools. Bilateral investigations are indeed possible. The key is to find the right people. Of course, there are risks but great synergies are to be had. Freeh and Falcone arranged to have their working relationship officially endorsed at the highest levels of their governments. An elaborate diplomatic ceremony was staged with meetings between the ministers of justice with speeches, signings of documents and pledges of mutual aid and good faith. They did so because they were working in uncharted waters. Certainly the U.S. was cooperating with foreign law enforcement agencies for decades. But nothing like a joint task for foreign law enforcement officials had ever been tried. So, in 1984 with great fanfare the Italian American Working Group against the Mafia was born and a new era in transatlantic law enforcement cooperation was launched (Martin 1998).

The break-through has shaped the U.S. International Crime Control Strategy. When Louis Freeh became Director of the FBI, the lesson he learned from Giovanni Falcone became the inspiration for the new global reach of the FBI. Freeh's philosophy was to find the Giovanni Falcones wherever they exist and to make allies of them. So in 1995, the FBI opened its International Law Enforcement Academy in Budapest where law enforcement officials from central and eastern Europe are being trained in American style techniques (Federal Bureau of Investigation 2000). Similar academies are being opened in Latin America and Asia.

Conclusion

The development of international law enforcement cooperation has occurred at about the same time in the United States and continental Europe. In both places the routes taken have followed similar trajectories; and in both cases, bureaucratic autonomy of police departments allowed them to initiate some efforts at international cooperation on their own. However, in America much more of those efforts have been driven from the bottom up while in continental Europe political elites have had a greater role in initiating changes.

The development of these institutions of police cooperation have been partially associated with two social processes, McDonaldization and implosion. McDonaldization refers to the process whereby certain extreme aspects of the development of bureaucratic efficiency are applied to more and more sectors of society. With regard to the institutions of international law enforcement cooperation, only two of the four dimensions of McDonaldization seem to apply. The development of internationalization of cooperation did involve promoting greater efficiency in basic police technology regarding communicating information about criminals; and it did require various forms of standardization of police work to make cooperation predictable. But, neither the control nor the calculability associated with McDonalization seems to be involved in the organization of international cooperation.

Clearly associated with the development of international law enforcement cooperation is the process of implosion, the disintegration of borders of all kinds: legal, jurisdictional, political, organizational, and technological. The world, which has always been borderless for bad guys, has become more borderless for cops. Implosion has involved the creation a new judicial space within which law enforcement agents of different countries can move without concern for the traditional limits on their authority. Implosion involves the blurring of immigration control, law enforcement, and espionage functions; the re-integration of high policing and low policing; the merging of databases into massive networks; the location of law enforcement officials in foreign countries; and the growth of binational strike forces.

While terrorism has been an important stimulus to greater international cooperation, it was not the lack of such cooperation that allowed September 11th to happen. It was a failure of cooperation among American agencies. The international response to September 11th is likely to bring stronger institutions of cooperation for fighting transnational crime and illegal immigration and some increase in efficiency in preventing terrorism. It is unlikely to resolve differences among states in terms of who they choose to define as terrorists.

Perennial obstacles to greater law enforcement cooperation are: differences over capital punishment, extradition, data protection, and the sharing of information. Notwithstanding these obstacles, the internationalization of criminal law enforcement is likely to reach a new high through such mechanisms as international joint task forces and updated mutual legal assistance treaties. It might be possible to negotiate new information sharing agreements in the post-September 11th atmosphere. But, the differences regarding capital punishment are not negotiable. Until capital punishment is abolished in the United States, it will be forced to work around gaps in its network of cooperative arrangements.

The terrorist attacks have hastened the implosion, the blurring of law enforcement and espionage functions; the linking of databases; and increasing extra-territorial policing. American federal law enforcement agents in particular now define their mission more in terms of prevention than prosecution. Reflecting on the Moussaoui case, the new American law enforcement thinking is that although searching Moussaoui's computer would have meant that he could not have been successfully prosecuted, it may have prevented the attacks; and, prevention of atrocities should be more important than prosecution of individuals. Thus, the firewall that once kept law enforcement and espionage activities apart has now been removed. Moreover, databases are being networked.

For America the history of international law enforcement cooperation reveals the many contradictions and inconsistencies in its experience. When European autocrats were inventing international police efforts to suppress political agitators trying to overthrow the feudal empires of Eastern Europe, the United States opened its door to the rebels. When France requested the extradition of a hardened criminal, America refused for the noblest reasons. Thomas Jefferson explained that America lacked faith in the fairness and justice of foreign criminal justice systems. He wrote:

> The laws of this country take no notice of crimes committed out of their jurisdiction. The most atrocious offender coming within their pale is received by them as an innocent man, and they have authorized no one to seize and deliver him. The evil of protecting malefactors of every dye is sensibly felt here as in other countries, but until a reformation of the criminal codes of most nations, to deliver fugitives from them would be become their accomplice,—the former, therefore, is viewed as the lesser evil (Dom. Letters, Vol. V., pp. 272-275; Mss. Dept. of State, as cited in Moore 1891:28).

Yet in the 1840s the United States demanded that Mexico extradite runaway slaves (Nadelmann 1993:41); and, today Mexico and European countries refuse to extradite criminals to or share evidence with the United States because they do not condone capital punishment.

Perhaps this history should be read as a hopeful lesson that things change. On the other hand, change itself is not necessarily for the better. Implosion and the McDonaldization of law enforcement may allow for more efficient responses to crime and terrorism but they raise the specter of the loss of privacy and the use of racial profiling.

NOTES

1 The attack in Madrid prompted the Council of the European Union to increase its commitment to international law enforcement coop-

eration made after the September 11th attacks. The Council declared that it was "[s]trengthening further the cooperation with the US and other partners in countering the threat posed by terrorism, [and] building on the solidarity and cooperation enshrined in the 2001 Plan of Action to Combat Terrorism..." (European Commission 2004:28).

2 The term, "European," overgeneralizes and hence is somewhat problematic. My references to "European" initiatives regarding law enforcement cooperation since the end of World War II refer to the joint efforts of European states in structuring the institutions of cooperation (such as the Trevi agreements and Europol) to fight terrorism and crime. My references to earlier developments are to happenings among the major continental countries, particularly Prussia and Germany, but not England.

3 In 1997 the District of Columbia's Criminal Justice Coordinating Council began development of an integrated data-sharing network. By 2001 such a network (JUSTIS) linked 17 databases to 13 federal and local public safety agencies. The decision to try to expand it to a regional system emerged out of a regular meeting of the system's advisory committee in July 2003. The target was to link DC to Virginia, Maryland, Pennsylvania and New York, all states victimized by the 911 attacks. The system has much greater functionality than the FBI's major system (NCIC). It is not limited to records of arrests for felonies. It includes real-time access to information about misdemeanors, traffic stops, case dispositions from the justice system, watch lists, escapes, photos and fingerprints. The program obtained funds from the Department of Homeland Security. But the initiative came from the bottom, from officials seeking better mousetraps, not from politicians seeking headlines. The regional network was established simply by contacting relevant mid-level officials in the target jurisdictions, soliciting their cooperation and ultimately getting their executives' approvals (interview with Earl L. Gillespie, Information Technology Liaison Officer, Washington, D.C., Aug. 20, 2003).

4 All EU member states have liaison officers posted abroad for a total of 300 officers. Half of them are stationed in Europe, mostly in other member states. The EU is considering entrusting liaison officers with responsibility for their own country but also for all the other countries of the Union as well (Statewatch 2001c). The EU is also planning greater use of joint (bilateral and multilateral) investigative teams (Statewatch 2001b).

5 A Dutch law enforcement officer once liaised to an anti-drug-trafficking effort in Colombia described how a half a dozen liaised officers from different countries were given office space in an embassy. He could walk down the hall and have direct communications with representatives the law enforcement interests of five other countries. While their first loyalty was to their homelands, the liaised officers developed a sense of themselves as a special group in its own right, an international posse out on some kind of frontier and going after the bad guys (Personal interview, March 2001, Dutch National Police, Zoetermeer, The Netherlands).

6 In the United States the use of joint federal, state and local task forces begun in the 1960s has been the main device through which local law enforcement has been linked into the efforts against organized crime networks in a direct way and is the way in which local police will be integrated into the post-September 11th counter-terrorism effort (Geller and Morris 1992; McGarrell and Schlegel 1993; McGee 2001; Gilmore Commission 2002).

7 Our request that the Office of International Affairs (OAI) of the Criminal Division, U.S. Department of Justice, make available statistics (not case information) based on its electronic database of case files was denied. OAI refused to use its limited resources for the task of compiling statistics not just for an individual researcher but also for purposes of creating a publishable annual report of activities.

The significance of this decision for researchers could not be greater. Foreign extraditions, requests for mutual legal assistance, and other transnational procedures all go through OAI. Such information is available online for other countries (see the updated

Bureau of Justice Statistics (BJS) World Factbook of Criminal Justice Systems at http://www.ojp.usdoj.gov/bjs/) One Latin American rapporteur preparing a contribution to the Factbook—which I was editing—felt threatened by the officials of the agencies from which he requested data.

8 The FBI did warn the Federal Aviation Administration about the possible threat but the FAA decided not to warn the airlines to increase security (Getler 2002).

9 Freer exchange of information between intelligence and law enforcement agencies had been recommended by the Commission on Terrorism whose report was issued only months before the September 11th attacks (U.S. National Commission on Terrorism 2000).

10 Two directors for counter-terrorism on the Clinton administration's National Security Council have given a chilling description of the lack of cooperation between the FBI and the Clinton White House. Every morning the two received a hundred or more reports from other federal intelligence sources but nothing from the FBI. They attribute it to the animus Director Louis Freeh had for President Clinton (Washington Post Staff Writer 2002a; Benjamin and Simon 2002). Of course, for much of his administration the FBI was investigating President Clinton.

On Sept. 16, George Tenet, CIA Director, issued a memo directing "that employees eliminate turf wars and cut out 'bureaucratic impediments to success' because intelligence handling 'must be absolutely seamless in waging this war, and we must lead'" (Pincus 2001).

11 The extradition of political offenders is an old and dicey proposition. The willingness of states to grant refuge and impunity to political agitators often depends on the nature of the political regime they oppose and the political ideology of the state offering refuge. At the 1898 Rome conference on international police cooperation the attendees adopted a Russian recommendation that they include

a clause in their extradition treaties providing that attacks on heads of state or their families be made grounds for extradition. The clause was rapidly adopted by governments in Europe. When the 1901 St. Petersburg conference was held, the Tsar's representatives proposed requiring governments to surrender all foreign political agitators on demand. Most European governments refused (Nadelmann 1992: IV-48).

At roughly the same period (1882) the United States modified its first immigration law passed in 1875 that had prohibited the importation of alien convicts. The new law provided that "all foreign convicts except those convicted of political offenses, upon arrival, shall be sent back to the nations to which they belong and from whence they came" (Clark 1969:162). The anarchists being prosecuted in central and eastern Europe were welcome in America.

In 1891 in America the liberal friends of the politically oppressed in other countries decided to clarify the coverage the political offense exception. They inserted into the next version of the law the phrase, "moral turpitude." As a result the revised category of people excluded from entry into the United States included "persons who had been convicted of a felony or other infamous crime or misdemeanor involving moral turpitude." The new law also explicitly stated that "nothing in this act shall be construed to exclude persons convicted of a political offense, notwithstanding the said political offense may be designated as a 'felony, crime, infamous crime, or misdemeanor involving moral inturpitude' by the laws of the land whence he came or the court convicting (Clark 1969:162). The phrase "moral turpitude," however, was never defined. Ironically, instead of providing a refuge for foreign political offenders, it placed enormous discretion in the hands of immigration officials who used it arbitrarily to exclude or deport deviants, minor offenders and people with political views judged to be radical (Van Vleck 1932; Clark 1969).

12 Excluding small regional police initiatives described by Benyon (1996:1061).

13 The head of the Unit on Police and Customs Cooperation of the European Commission, Willem Aldershoff, has no law enforcement

experience and regards it as an unnecessary qualification for his position (Interview, Brussels, June 27, 2001).

14 Jensen (1981) credits the work of the Rome and the St. Petersburg conferences with transforming the European response to transnational anarchist violence from one that was essentially political to one in which the technological and bureaucratic dimensions of police cooperation could be addressed in practical terms. This, he argues, laid the groundwork for the establishment in 1923 of the International Criminal Police Commission (ICPC), forerunner of INTERPOL.

15 The name Interpol began to be used after the Second World War when ICPC's Secretary-General referred to the organization by its cable address in press conferences. In 1956 the formal name was changed to the International Criminal Police Organization-Interpol (Fooner 1973:27).

16 Since World War II various forms of law enforcement and judicial cooperative arrangements among European states emerged. Some germinated from regional ties such as those among the Nordic countries and those among the Benelux countries. Others grew out of common law enforcement interests such as the Cross-Channel Police Intelligence Conferences related to the construction of the channel tunnel; the meetings of the Heads of Drugs Squads of European capitals; and the Police Working Group on Terrorism. Most were linked to the larger European project whose central focus was the economic integration of the entire region. The free movement of goods, capital and labor among member states required new security arrangements and methods for law enforcement.

17 Interpol agreed to the appointment of a few liaison officers at its headquarters to help coordinate the anti-drug campaign (Fijnaut 1987:39).

18 Interview with Emanuel Marotta, Deputy Director, Europol, March 2001, The Hague.

19 Europol may participate in a "support" role in joint investigations with police agencies of member states and may request member states to initiate investigations (Council of Europe 2002b).

20 To Europeans capital punishment is regarded as an abuse on a par with torture and genocide. All three are banned by the European Convention on Human Rights signed by 34 countries.

21 George W. Bush is also disdained by many Europeans for his close identification with capital punishment. "He's the world champion executioner," said Robert Badinter, the former French justice minister. "He is a horrible symbol of your mania for the death penalty." Claudia Roth, a member of the German Parliament, expressed it this way: "What we know about the new president, is just two things. He is the son of President Bush, and he has sent 150 people to their death in Texas, including the mentally ill" (Reid 2000).

REFERENCES

Alderson, J.C. and W.A. Tupman, eds. 1990. *Policing Europe After 1992.* Proceedings of an International Seminar Held at the University of Exeter April 4-7, 1989. Exeter: University of Exeter, Centre for Police Studies.

Anderson, Malcolm. 1989. *Policing the World: Interpol and the Politics of International Police Co-Operation.* Oxford: Clarendon Press.

_____. 2000a. "Counter-terrorism as an Objective of European Police Cooperation." In *European Democracies Against Terrorism: Governmental Policies and Intergovernmental Cooperation*, edited by F. Reinares. Brookfield, Vt.: Ashgate.

Anderson, Malcolm, Joanna Apap, and Christopher Mulkins, eds. 2001. *Policy Alternatives to Schengen Border Controls on the Future EU External Frontier.* Proceedings of an Expert Seminar, February 23-24, Brussels: Center for European Policy Studies.

Anderson, Malcolm, Didier Bigo, and Eberhard Bort. 2000b. "Frontiers, Identity and Security in Europe: An Agenda for Research." In *Borderlands Under Stress*, edited by M. Pratt and J.A. Brown. The Hague; Boston: Kluwer Law International.

Anderson, Malcolm and Monica den Boer, eds. 1992. *European Police Co-Operation: Proceedings of a Seminar.* Project Group European Police Co-operation. Edinburgh: University of Edinburgh, Department of Politics.

_____. 1994. *Policing Across National Boundaries.* London: Pinter Publishers.

Baudrillard, Jean. 1983. "Simulations." *Foreign Agents Series.* New York, N.Y., U.S.A.: Semiotext(e), Inc.

Benjamin, Daniel and Steven Simon. 2002. *The Age of Sacred Terror.* New York: Random House.

Benyon, John. 1996. "European Citizenship and European Union Justice and Home Affairs." In *Building Police Cooperation: The European Construction Site Around the Third Pillar.* Center for the Study of Public Order. University of Leicester. Retrieved Sept. 16, 2002 (www.psa.uk/cps/1996/beny.pdf).

———. 1997. "The Developing System of Police Cooperation in the European Union." In *Crime and Law Enforcement in the Global Community*, edited by W.F. McDonald. Cincinnati, OH: Anderson Publishers.

Benyon, John, Lynne Turnbull, Andrew Willis, Rachel Woodward, and Adrian Beck. 1993. *Police Co-Operation in Europe: An Investigation.* Leicester: Centre for the Study of Public Order. University of Leicester.

Berkowitz, Bruce. 2003. "The Big Difference Between Intelligence and Evidence." *The Washington Post*, Feb. 2, p. B01.

Bigo, Didier. 1994. "The European Internal Security Field: Stakes and Rivalries in a Newly Developing Area of Police Intervention." In *Policing Across National Boundaries*, edited by M. Anderson and M. . London: Pinter.

Birch, Roger. 1989. "Policing in Europe in 1992." *The Police Journal* 62(July):203-10.

Brodeur, J.P. 1983. "High Policing and Low Policing: Remarks about the Policing of Political Activities." *Social Problems* 3(5):507-20.

Camarota, Steven A. 2002. *The Open Door: How Militant Islamic Terrorists Entered and Remained in the United States, 1993-2001.* Center for Immigration Studies. Available at (http://www.cis.org/articles/2002/terrorism.html).

Camilleri, Joseph A. and Jim Falk. 1992. *End of Sovereignty? The Politics of a Shrinking and Fragmenting World.* Aldershot, Hants, England; Brookfield, Vt.: Elgar.

Clark, Jane P. 1969[1931]. *Deportation of Aliens from the United States to Europe.* New York, N.Y.: Arno Press and The New York Times.

Clymer, Adam. 2001. "Lawmakers Want C.I.A. to Share Data on Foreigners," *The New York Times*, Nov. 2.

Collins, Mike. 2004. "Dismantling 'the Wall.'" Letters to the Editor, *The Washington Post*, April 26, p. A22.

Council of Europe. 2001. "Euopol Convention: European Police Office" (Official Journal No C 316, 27.11.1995). In *Europa: Activities of the European Union: Summaries of Legislation: Area of Security.* European Union. Retrieved Sept. 30, 2002 (http://europa.eu.int/scadplus/leg/en/lvb/l14005b.htm).

_____. 2002a. Justice and Home Affairs, *Council Decision of 28 February 2002 Setting up Eurojust with a View to Reinforcing the Fight Against Serious Crime,* June 3.

_____. 2002b. Presidency, *Note: Council Act Drawing up a Protocol Amending the Convention on the Establishment of a European Police Office (Europol Convention)12340/02 EUROPOL 70,* Sept. 25.

_____. 2002c. *Presidency, Request for a Negotiation Mandate for the Presidency on Judicial Cooperation in Criminal Matters on the Basis of Articles 38 and 24 TEU6438/1/02 REV 1 EXT 1 CATS 5 USA 4,*May 23.

_____. Justice and Home Affairs. 1999. "Council Act of 3 November 1998 Adopting Rules Applicable to Europol Analysis Files." *Official Journal C 026*, Jan. 30:0001-0009.

Deflem, Mathieu. 1996. "International Policing in Nineteenth-Century Europe: The Police Union of German States, 1851-1866." *International Criminal Justice Review* 6:36-57.

———. 2002a. "Technology and the Internationalization of Policing: A Comparative-Historical Perspective." *Justice Quarterly* 19(3):454-75.

———. 2002b. *Policing World Society.* Oxford: Oxford University Press.

Diamond, John. 2002. "Shackles Loosened on U.S. Intelligence." *USATODAY.Com*, July 9. Retrieved 03/05/2004 (http://www.usatoday.com/news/washington/2002/07/09/intelligence.htm).

Eaton, Trace. 1993. "Wanted for Murder: Many Find Haven in Mexico." *Orange County (CA) Register*, Feb. 14.

Eggen, Dan. 2002a. "Agent Claims FBI Supervisor Thwarted Probe: Stopping Some Hijackers Said Possible," *The Washington Post*, May 27, p. A01.

———. 2002b. "Airports Screened Nine of Sept. 11 Hijackers," *The Washington Post*, March 2, p. A11.

———. 2002c. "FBI Pigeonholed Agent's Request: Canvassing of Flight Schools For Al Qaeda Was Rejected," *The Washington Post*, May 22, p. A01.

———. 2002d. "Moussaoui Probe Pushed U.S. Limits; FBI Wanted to Deport Suspect to France to Access His Computer," *The Washington Post*, Jan. 31, p. A1.

Eggen, Dan and Bill Miller. 2002. "FBI Memo's Details Raise New Questions," *The Washington Post*, May 19, p. A01.

Eggen, Dan and Dana Priest. 2002. "FBI Agent Urged Search for Hijacker: Request Was Turned Down Before Attacks, Panel Is Told," *The Washington Post*, Sept. 21, p. A01.

Commission Staff, European Commission, *Compendium Counter Terrorism Actions: Contributions of the Commission Services May 25* (2004). Brussels.

Federal Bureau of Investigation, U.S. Department of Justice. 2000. "FBI History: A Time Line." Retrieved October 11, 2000 (http://www.fbi.gov/yourfbi/history/90years/90years1.htm).

Fijnaut, Cyrille. 1987. "The Internationalization of Criminal Investigation in Western Europe." In *Police Cooperation in Europe: Lectures at the International Symposium on Surveillance*, edited by C. Fijnaut and R. Hermans. Lochem: Van den Brink.

———. 1993. *The Internationalization of Police Cooperation in Western Europe*. SMP Cahier. Boston, MA: Kluwer.

Fijnaut, Cyrille and Gary T Marx. 1995. *Undercover Police Surveillance in Comparative Perspective*. Norwell, MA: Kluwer Academic Publishers.

Fischer, Howard. 2002. "Ashcroft Defends Anti-Terror Plan." *The Associated Press* (Phoenix), May 8. Available at (http://Www.Azstarnet.Com/Star/Wed/20508ashcroft.html).

Fooner, Michael. 1973. *Interpol: The Inside Story of the International Crime-Fighting Organization*. Chicago, IL: H. Regnery Co.

———. 1975. *Inside Interpol: Combating World Crime Through Science and International Police Cooperation*. New York: Coward, McCann and Geoghegan.

Fosdick, Raymond P. 1915. *European Police Systems*. New York: The Century Co.

Gates, Daryl F. and Keith E. Ross. 1990. "Foreign Prosecution Liaison Unit Helps Apprehend Suspects Across the Border." *The Police Chief* April:153-54.

Geller, William A. and Norval Morris. 1992. "Relations Between Federal and Local Police." In *Crime and Justice*, vol. 15, *Modern Policing*, edited by M. Tonry and N. Morris. Chicago, IL: University of Chicago Press.

Gerth, Jeff. 2003. "C.I.A. Chief Won't Name Officials Who Failed to Put Hijackers on Watch List Not Named," *The New York Times*, May 15, p. A25.

Getler, Michael. 2002. "The 'First Rough Draft,'" *The Washington Post*, May 26, p. B06.

Gilmore Commission. "Advisory Panel to Assess Domestic Response Capabilities for Terrorism Involving Weapons of Mass Destruction." 2002. Fourth Annual Report to the President and the Congress. Santa Monica, CA: Rand. Retrieved 22/01/2003 (http://www.rand.org/nsrd/terrpanel/terror4.pdf).

Gugliotta, Guy and Jonathan Krim. 2001. "Push for Increased Surveillance Powers Worries Some," *The Washington Post*, Sept. 25, p. A04.

Guardian. 2002. "Ninth Arrest in Terror Investigation." *The Guardian Unlimited (London)*, Jan. 18. Retrieved July 6, 2004 (http://www.guardian.co.uk/Archive/Article/0,4273,4338042,00.html).

Hsu, Spencer S. 2003. "Crossing Lines to Fight Terrorism: D.C., Four States to Share Law Enforcement, Other Records," *The Washington Post*, Aug. 6, Metro, p. B02.

Isikoff, Michael. 2002. "Unheeded Warnings: FBI Agent's Notes Pointed to Possible World Trade Center Attack," *Newsweek*, May 20. Available at (http://Www.Msnbc.Com/News/751100.Asp).

Jacobson, David. 1996. *Rights Across Borders: Immigration and the Decline of Citizenship*. Baltimore, MD: The Johns Hopkins Press.

Jensen, Richard Back. 1981. "The International Anti-Anarchist Conference of 1898 and the Origins of Interpol." *Journal of Contemporary History* 16(April):323-47.

Johnston, David. 2002. "Pre-Attack Memo Cited Bin Laden," *The New York Times*, May 15.

Kurtz, Howard. 2002. "The 9/11 Blame Game," *The Washington Post*, May 16.

Lane, Roger. 1971. *Policing the City: Boston, 1822-1885*. New York, NY: Atheneum.

Lee, Mike and Diane Smith. 2001. "'A Wounded Agency.' Lapses, Workload Prompt Calls for INS Overhaul." *The Fort Worth Star-Telegram*, Nov. 4, p. 33.

Liang, Hsi-Huey. 1992. *The Rise of Modern Police and the European State System from Metternich to the Second World War*. Cambridge: Cambridge University Press.

_____. 1980. "International Cooperation of Political Police in Europe, 1815-1914." *Mitteilugen Des Osterreichischen Staatsarchivs* 33:193-217.

Lichtblau, Eric and Adam Liptak. 2003. "On Terror, Spying and Guns, Ashcroft Expands Reach," *The New York Times*, Mar. 15, p. A01.

Loeb, Vernon. 2002. "Beyond the Blame Game," *Washingtonpost.Com*, Sept. 9. Retrieved Sept. 13, 2002 (http://www.washingtonpost.com/wp-dyn/articles/A56650-2002Sep9.html).

Loschiavo, N.J. 1975. "Law Enforcement Intelligence Unit." *Police Chief* 62(Feb. 2):46, 82.

MAGLOCEN. 1996. *1996 Annual Report*. Middle Atlantic-Great Lakes Organized Crime Law Enforcement Network. Newton, PA.

Martin, Richard A. 1990-1991. "Problems in International Law Enforcement." *Fordham International Law Journal* 14:519.

_____. 1998. "The Italian-American Working Group: Why It Worked." A Paper of The Working Group on Organized Crime. Washington, DC: National Strategy Information Center.

McDonald, William F. 1997. "Crime and Justice in the Global Village: Towards Global Criminology." In *Crime and Law Enforcement in the Global Village*, edited by W.F. McDonald. Cincinnati, OH: Anderson Publishers.

_____. 1999. "The Changing Boundaries of Law Enforcement: State and Local Law Enforcement, Illegal Immigration and Transnational Crime Control: Final Report." Washington, DC: National Institute of Justice. Unpublished report.

McDonnell, Patrick J. 1996. "Law Could Alter Role of Police on Immigration," *Los Angeles Times*, Sept. 30, p. A01.

McGarrell, E.F and K Schlegel. 1993. "Implementation of Federally Funded Multi-Jurisdictional Drug Task Forces: Organizational Structure and Interagency Relationships." *Journal of Criminal Justice* 21(3):231-44.

McGee, Jim. 2001. "Joint Task Force Became Model of Counter-terrorism," *The Washington Post*, Nov. 28, p. A14.

_____. 2002. "Fighting Terror With Databases: Domestic Intelligence Plans Stir Concern," *The Washington Post*, Feb. 16, p. A27.

McGillis, Daniel. 1996. *Overview of Federal International Justice Assistance Efforts*. Research Applications Review, July. Washington, DC: National Institute of Justice, U.S. Department of Justice.

McMahon, Maeve. 1997. "The McDonaldization of Criminal Justice: North American Reflections on an International Trend." Presented at the XXVth Annual Conference of the European Group for the Study of Deviance and Social Control, Sept., Kazimierz, Poland.

Miller, Bill and Dan Eggen. 2002. "FBI Culture Blamed for Missteps on Moussaoui: Agent Says 'Climate Of Fear' Hurt Probe," *The Washington Post*, May 25, p. A01.

Miller, John. 2002. "Early Warnings: Pre-Sept. 11 Cautions Went Unheeded," *ABCNews*, Feb. 18. Retrieved Feb. 19, 2002 (http://printerfriendly.abcnews.com/printerfriendly/Print?fetchFromGLUE=true&GLUEService=ABCNewsCom).

Moore, John Bassett. 1891. *A Treatise on Extradition and Interstate Rendition*. Boston: Boston Book Company.

Nadelmann, Ethan A. 1992. "Criminalization and Crime Control in International Society." Unpublished manuscript cited with permission.

_____. 1993. *Cops Across Borders: The Internationalization of U.S. Criminal Law Enforcement*. University Park, PA: The Pennsylvania State University Press.

National Commission on Terrorism Attacks Against the United States. 2004. "Reforming Law Enforcement, Counter-terrorism and Intelligence Collection in the United States." (Staff Statement No. 12). Retrieved June 17, 2004 (http://www.9-11commission.gov/hearings/hearing10/staff_statement_12.pdf).

Nepote, Jean. 1977. "Interpol: The Development of International Policing." In *Pioneers in Policing*, edited by P.J. Stead. Montclair, N.J.: Patterson Smith.

Norton-Taylor, Richard. 2002. "Secret Terror Treaty Plan Raises Rights Fears," *The Guardian* (London), Sept. 3, p. 1.

O'Harrow Jr., Robert. 2003. "U.S. Backs Florida's New Counter-terrorism Database: 'Matrix' Offers Law Agencies Faster Access to Americans' Personal Records to Americans' Personal Records to Americans' Personal Records," *The Washington Post*, Aug. 6, p. A01.

Pincus, Walter. 2001. "CIA Steps Up Scope, Pace Of Efforts On Terrorism: Intelligence Agencies Focus on Cooperation," *The Washington Post*, Oct. 9, p. A04.

Pratt, Martin and Janet Allison Brown. 2000. "Borderlands Under Stress." *International Boundary Studies Series*. The Hague; Boston: Kluwer Law International.

President's Commission on Law Enforcement and Administration of Justice. 1967a. *The Challenge of Crime in a Free Society*. Washington, DC: Government Printing Office.

Priest, Dana and Dan Eggen. 2002a. "9/11 Probers Say Agencies Failed to Heed Attack Signs," *The Washington Post*, Sept. 19, p. A01.

———. 2002b. "FBI Faulted on Al Qaeda Assessment: Domestic Threat was Underestimated, Panel Told," *The Washington Post*, Sept. 20, p. A01.

Reid, T.R. 2000. "Many Europeans See Bush as Executioner," *The Washington Post*, Dec. 17, p. A36.

Ritzer, George. 2000. *The McDonaldization of Society*. Thousand Oaks, CA: Pine Forge Press.

_____. ed. 2003. *McDonaldization: The Reader*. Thousand Oaks, CA: Pine Forge Press.

Robinson, Matthew B. 2003. "The McDonaldization of America's Police, Courts and Corrections." In *McDonaldization: The Reader*, edited by G. Ritzer. Thousand Oaks, CA: Pine Forge Press.

Ross, Brian. 2002. "U.S. Targets Overlooked: FBI Ignored Warnings From Flight Schools; Missed Two Al Qaeda Terrorists." *ABC Nightly News*, Feb. 20. Retrieved March 3, 2002 (http://abcnews.go.com/sections/wnt/DailyNews/missedsignals_3_020220.html).

Rupprecht, Reinhard. 1993. "Internationalization of Police Cooperation in Western Europe: The German Perspective." In *The Internationalization of Police Cooperation in Western Europe*, edited by C. Fijnaut. Boston, MA: Kluwer.

Salant, Jonathan D. 2002. "FAA Warned of Bin Laden in 1998," *Associated Press Online*, May 27.

Sassen, Saskia. 1996. *Losing Control? Sovereignty in an Age of Globalization*. New York: Columbia University Press.

Schmidt, Susan. 2002. "Lawyers For FBI Faulted In Search: Panel Told Legal Staff Misunderstood FISA," *The Washington Post*, Sept. 25, p. A12.

Schmidt, Susan and Dan Eggen. 2002. "Suspected Planner of 9/11 Attacks Captured in Pakistan After Gunfight," *The Washington Post*, Sept. 14, p. A01.

Sheptycki, James W.E. 1995. "Transnational Policing and the Makings of a Postmodern State." *British Journal of Criminology* 35(4):613-36.

———. 1997. "Transnationalism, Crime Control and the European State System: A Review of the Literature." *International Criminal Justice Review* 7:130-40.

Sheridan, Mary Beth. 2001. "Suspects Slipped Past Consulates' Screening," *The Washington Post*, Oct. 5, p. A14.

Shichor, David. 1997. "Three Strikes as a Public Policy: The Convergence of the New Penology and the McDonaldization of Punishment." *Crime and Delinquency* 43(4):470-93.

Smith Jr., Bruce. 1960. *Police Systems in the United States*. 2d ed. New York: Harper Row.

Statewatch. 2000. "European Public Prosecutions Unit Created." (Semdoc May 2001). *Statewatch Bulletin* 10(3 & 4). Retrieved Oct. 2, 2002 (http://www.statewatch.org/semdoc/index.html).

_____. 2001a. "Amsterdam Police Raid Linked to ETA—and 'Eurojust.'" (Statewatch News Online). Retrieved Oct. 2, 2002 (http://www.statewatch.org/semdoc/index.html).

_____. 2001b. "EU Joint Investigation Teams: Scope Changed from Tracking Terrorism, Drugs and Illegal Immgration." *SEMDOC*, June. Retrieved July 2, 2002 (http://www.statewatch.org/semdoc/).

_____. 2001c. "Liaison Officers: Global Policing?" *SEMDOC*, April. Retrieved July 2, 2002 (http://www.statewatch.org/semdoc/).

_____. 2002a. "The Activities and Development of Europol: Towards an Unaccountable FBI in Europe." *SEMDOC*, Feb. 7. Retrieved July 2, 2002 (http://www.statewatch.org/semdoc/).

_____. 2002b. "EU Negotiating Secret Agreement with US on Judicial Cooperation in Criminal Matters." *SEMDOC*, March 13. Retrieved July 2, 2002 (http://www.statewatch.org/semdoc/).

_____. 2002c. "Europol: More Powers, Less Democratic Control." *SEMDOC*, June. Retrieved July 2, 2002 (http://www.statewatch.org/semdoc/).

———. 2002d. "Secret EU-US Agreement on Criminal Cooperation Being Negotiated" (Analysis #12). Statewatch. Retrieved Oct. 2, 2002 (http://www.statewatch.org/news/2002/aug/analy12.pdf).

_____. 2002e. "Spain and Italy Pioneer a 'Common Area of Security and Justice." (Semdoc Summary. Access by Subscription.) Statewatch. Retrieved Oct. 18, 2002 (http://www.statewatch.org/semdoc/).

_____.2002f. (Semdoc). Retrieved Oct. 2, 2002 (http://www.statewatch.org /news/2002/feb/useu.pdf).

Struck, Doug, Howard Schneider, Karl Vick, and Peter Baker. 2001. "Borderless Network of Terror: Bin Laden Followers Reach Across Globe," *The Washington Post*, Sept. 23, p. A01.

U.S. National Commission on Terrorism. 2000. *Countering the Changing Threat of International Terrorism*. Washington, D.C.: Government Printing Office.

United Nations. General Assembly. 1990. *Model Treaty on Mutual Legal Assistance in Criminal Matters Adopted by the General Assembly as resolution 45/117 on the recommendation of the Eighth Congress on the Prevention of Crime and the Treatment of Offenders on the 14 December 1990)*. New York, N.Y.

United States Congress. Senate Select Committee on Intelligence and the House Permanent Select Committee on Intelligence. 2002. Joint Intelligence Committee Inquiry into September 11th Terrorist Attacks. *Joint Inquiry Staff Statement, Part I, Staff Director's Statement to the Joint Committee, Sept. 18, 2002*, 107 Cong.

Van Vleck, William C. 1932. *The Administrative Control of Aliens: A Study in Administrative Law and Procedure*. New York: The Commonwealth Fund.

Vise, David A. 2000. "New Global Role Puts FBI in Unsavory Company," *The Washington Post*, Oct. 29, p. A1.

Walker, Samuel. 1977. *A Critical History of Police Reform: The Emergence of Professionalism*. Lexington, MA: Lexington Books.

Washington Post Editorial. 2004. "Mr. Ashcroft's Smear," *The Washington Post*, April 20, p. A18.

Washington Post Staff Writer. 2002a. "Anti-Terror War's Missteps Detailed By Ex-NSC Staffers: Clinton Aides' Book Cites Turf Wars," *The Washington Post*, Oct. 2, p. A06.

_____. 2002b. "Lost Chance on Terrorists Cited: INS, FAA Might Have Found 2 of 19 Hijackers, Officials Say," *The Washington Post*, Oct. 2, p. A01.

Weber, Max. 1976. *The Protestant Ethic and the Spirit of Capitalism*. 2d ed. Translated by T. Parsons. London: Allen and Unwin.

Wilkinson, Paul. 1985. "European Police Cooperation." In *Police and Public Order in Europe*, edited by J. Roach and J. Thomaneck. London Dover, N.H.: Croom Helm.

Will, George F. 2001. "A Different FBI?" *The Washington Post*, Oct. 14, p. B07.

Williams, Daniel. 2002. "15 Men Held in Italy Face Terror Charges Based on U.S. Tip," *The Washington Post*, Sept. 13, p. A22.

Winer, Jonathan. 1998. "Some Possible Topics for Academic Research in Transnational Crime." Presented at the American Society of Criminology, Nov. 13, Washington, DC.

ABOUT THE AUTHORS

Jay Albanese is Chief of the International Center at the National Institute of Justice. He is on leave from his position as professor of Government & Public Policy at Virginia Commonwealth University. He holds a Ph.D. from the School of Criminal Justice at Rutgers University. He is a past president of the Academy of Criminal Justice Sciences (ACJS), and is currently Executive Director of the International Association for the Study of Organized Crime (www.iasoc.net). Dr. Albanese is the author of books that include *Criminal Justice* (3rd edition, Allyn & Bacon 2005), *Organized Crime in Our Times* (Lexis Nexis/Anderson 2004), and is co-editor of *Organized Crime: World Perspectives* (Prentice Hall 2003).

Rosemary Barberet is Ramón y Cajal Research Fellow in the Department of Political Science and Sociology, Universidad Carlos III, Madrid, Spain. Previous academic appointments include the University of Leicester, England, the Universidad de Sevilla and the Universidad de Castilla-La Mancha, Spain. She has taught research methods to criminology students since 1990. Her research has centered on self-reported delinquency, violence against women, victimization and crime indicators. She is in her second elected term as Chair of the Division of International Criminology of the American Society of Criminology.

Heather Clawson is Managing Associate with Caliber Associates, Inc., and was the Principal Investigator for the *Needs Assessment of Service Providers and Trafficking Victims* and is Principal Investigator for the *Evaluation of Office for Victims of Crime Comprehensive Services Trafficking Grantees*. Currently Dr. Clawson also evaluates human trafficking training programs and serves as an advisory group member for the development of an interdisciplinary training for human trafficking.

Jennifer Schrock Donnelly is an International Program Specialist with the International Center, National Institute of Justice, U.S. Department of Justice. She holds a Master of Science in Justice, Law and Society from the School of Public Affairs at the American University in Washington, D.C. Publications include "Women in the Criminal Justice System," and *The Prediction and Control of Organized Crime: The Experience of Post-Soviet Ukraine* (Transaction 2004).

Ellen Go is Research Associate with Caliber Associates, Inc., and played a critical role in the *Needs Assessment of Service Providers and Trafficking Victims*, and currently assists in the *Evaluation of Office for Victims of Crime Comprehensive Services Trafficking Grantees*, and an evaluation of human trafficking training programs. Also, she is part of a team providing technical assistance to OVC trafficking grantees. Ms. Go holds a B.A. in Sociology from Yale University.

Talene L. Kelegian is a graduate of Boston University in Boston, Massachusetts. She holds a Bachelor of Arts degree with concentrations in Sociology and Religion. Talene worked with the Drugs and Crime and International Research Division, National Institute of Justice in 2003. She is currently working as a Residential Counselor with Charles River ARC in Needham, Massachusetts.

William F. McDonald is Professor of Sociology and Anthropology, and Deputy Director, Institute of Criminal Law and Procedure, Georgetown University. He received his D.Crim. from the University of California, Berkeley; his M.Ed. from Boston College and his B.A. from the University of Notre Dame. The subjects he has taught since 1970 include criminology; criminal justice; research methods and statistics; and comparative criminal justice systems. His published work include edited books on the globalization of law enforcement; the victim; plea bargaining; the prosecutor; and criminal defense counsel; 50 authored and co-authored monographs and articles on sentencing; police-prosecutor relationships; illegal immigration; pretrial release; drug law enforcement; and comparative criminal justice.

Bradley Myles is a Research Assistant with Caliber Associates, Inc. His areas of focus include human trafficking, victim services, transnational crime, and at-risk youth and families. Mr. Myles has contributed to project team efforts for the *Needs Assessment of Service Providers and Trafficking Victims* and the *Evaluation of Office for Victims of Crime Comprehensive Services Trafficking Grantees*. He holds a B.A. in Political Science and a B.A. in Psychology from Stanford University.

Hedi Nasheri is an Associate Professor of Justice Studies at Kent State University and a Visiting Fellow at the University of London's Institute of

Advanced Legal Studies in the U.K. She received her graduate training in social policy and law (Ph.D. 1992) from Case Western Reserve University. She is the author of several books including *Economic Espionage and Industrial Spying* (Cambridge University Press 2004) and numerous journal articles and book reviews. She has written and lectured extensively in the areas of law and social sciences and has given a number of invited lectures nationally and internationally on a wide range of policy and law related topics. Professor Nasheri's research interests pertain to four related topics: Law & Technology, Protection of Trade Secrets & Economic Espionage, Cyber-Crimes, and Comparative Jurisprudence.

Dina Siegel is an Assistant Professor at the Department of Criminology and Criminal Law, Vrije Universiteit Amsterdam. She studied sociology and social anthropology at the Tel-Aviv University, Israel and obtained her Ph.D. in cultural anthropology at the Vrije Universiteit of Amsterdam, the Netherlands. She has studied and published several articles on post-Soviet organized crime, terrorism, women trafficking, criminality in diamond sector, and more recently on XTC distribution and XTC policy in the Netherlands. She conducted ethnographic research on Russian-speaking criminals in the Netherlands, *Russian biznes in the Netherlands* (2002). She is currently studying Israeli organized crime in the Netherlands and Belgium.

Kevonne Small is a Research Associate with Caliber Associates, Inc., and has managed several projects on transnational crime, human trafficking, and victim services for the Office of Victims of Crime and the National Institute of Justice. She holds a J.D. from Villanova University School of Law and is currently working on her Ph.D. in Justice, Law & Society at American University on quality of life and crime.

A

B

C

D

I

J

K

L

M

N

O

P

R

S

U

V

W

Y

Z

Printed in the United States
26206LVS00003B/1-74

9 781897 160053